Henry Crawford Dorr

The Properties of Providence

And their controversies with the freeholders

Henry Crawford Dorr

The Properties of Providence
And their controversies with the freeholders

ISBN/EAN: 9783337402914

Printed in Europe, USA, Canada, Australia, Japan

Cover: Foto ©Suzi / pixelio.de

More available books at **www.hansebooks.com**

COLLECTIONS

OF THE

Rhode Island Historical Society.

VOLUME IX.

PROVIDENCE, RHODE ISLAND.

1897.

THE PROPRIETORS OF PROVIDENCE,

AND THEIR

CONTROVERSIES WITH THE FREEHOLDERS.

BY

HENRY C. DORR.

COMMITTEE ON PUBLICATIONS.

At the annual meeting of the Rhode Island Historical Society, January 12, 1897, it was voted : —

"That the Publication Committee be and is hereby authorized and instructed to publish the paper of Mr. Henry C. Dorr, on the "Controversy between the Proprietors and the Freeholders of Providence," as Vol. IX. of the Society's Collections, together with such preface and index as are approved by Mr. Dorr ; also,

"That the thanks of the Society be extended to Mr. Dorr for this valuable contribution to the early history of the Providence Plantations, and also to those members of the Society who defray the expense of this publication."

THE PROPRIETORS OF PROVIDENCE, AND THEIR CONTROVERSIES WITH THE FREEHOLDERS.

CONTENTS.

	PAGES.
THE PECULIAR TITLE TO THE LANDS,	1–11
THE "INITIAL DEED,"	12–20
THE ARBITRATORS' PROPOSALS FOR A FORM OF GOVERNMENT,	21–26
SAMUEL GORTON IN PROVIDENCE,	27–32
SECESSION AT PAWTUXET,	33–35
PROGRESS UNDER THE CHARTER OF 1644,	36–56
ENDEAVORS OF VANE AND WILLIAMS,	57–64
THE PROPRIETORS' CLAIM TO LANDS WEST OF THE INDIAN LINE,	65–72
THE CONTROVERSY OF WILLIAMS AND HARRIS,	73–77
THE SACHEMS CONFIRM THE GRANTS; FREEMEN AND PURCHASERS,	78–86
THE "SEVEN-MILE LINE" AND THE "FOUR-MILE LINE,"	86–95
NEW CONTENTIONS UNDER THE NEW CHARTER,	95–104
INDIAN WARS; THE PROPRIETORS BECOME A CORPORATION,	104–113
GROWTH UNDER THE PROPRIETORS,	113–128
SUMMARY AND CONCLUSIONS,	128–136

THE PROPRIETORS OF PROVIDENCE, AND THEIR CONTROVERSIES WITH THE FREEHOLDERS.

The earliest controversy of the Plantations was between the Proprietors and the Freeholders. During two generations it disturbed the quiet of the town meeting and the harmony of private life, and, more than anything beside, delayed union and success. It arose out of the peculiar title to the lands. Its ill consequences long survived it. Its details are now forgotten, and many of its historical records have perished. But it is worthy of remembrance, if only as an illustration of the fact, that of all political blunders, those of the founders of a State are the most permanent in influence and the most difficult of remedy.

The troubles of the townsmen had a beginning earlier than the Plantation itself. Such an undertaking requires, and has everywhere else received, forethought, organization, and resources. It cannot be extemporized, or adventured suddenly and in haste. Such was Williams's own view of his project. While yet a resident of Plymouth (1631–32), he had known Canonicus, and had received assurance of the favor and aid of the great Sachem of the Narragansetts. Williams then contemplated a settlement at Acquetneck, and had ever since been occupied in slowly maturing his scheme. Sometimes he thought of going alone into the wilderness, as to a mission to do good to the natives' souls.* A little reflection must have taught him that this was but a day-dream. He must have seen that with such a country and such a bay, neither England, France, Holland nor Massachusetts would very long

*"My soul's desire was, to do the natives good." Answer of Roger Williams to the Declaration of William Harris against the Town of Providence, p. 53, Rider's Hist. Tract No. 14.

leave him alone in Narragansett. At the time of his banishment, Williams had no definite scheme for his colony. The
controversial temper which he had manifested did not attract
the organizing spirits of Massachusetts to any enterprise
which was to be subject to his control. He had need to consult with men of liberal views in England, for England was
not wholly Puritan. These could have aided him with capital'
with men skilled in mechanic arts, and with those competent
to found and to conduct a system of education which was,
most of all, needed in such a colony as he proposed. While
he was slowly developing his plans, he suddenly received
news of an order for his arrest. He saw that his last opportunity had come. Had he waited until his return from London
he would have found the only refuge in New England closed
against him by Massachusetts.* [See his letter to Mason,
1670.] He says that he lost £1000 by the breaking up of his
business. His arrangements of his private affairs must be
made upon the instant. Directions must be given at once for
the conduct of a trading-house, very considerable for those
days. His family must be provided with temporary support,
and his leave-taking with such of his friends as could be
assembled must be gone through. The colony at Mooshassuc was founded within six hours. All these arrangements
were hurried through during one short winter day, and he
went forth alone and unprovided, into the winter night, no
one knew whither. He could be assured of the companionship
of but few who could be of service to his undertaking. During the next spring, he was pressed with the labor of planting
at Seekonk. He had little leisure and few facilities for correspondence, and but few men fit to plan a new social organization. Some whom he asked or permitted to follow him, he
would not have invited had he known them better, for they
certainly were of little use. Some, well qualified for the
work, were probably dissuaded from it by their knowledge
that beside the terror of the wilderness they must encounter
the hostility of Massachusetts, and the loss of old friendships

---

*Williams was not expecting a speedy removal to R. I. at the time of
his banishment, and had made no preparations for it.

there.   A departure to Mooshassuc seems to have been regarded among "the Bay people," very much as the men of
this generation looked upon a settlement in Utah.

Had Williams been able to collect his substance, and to
mature his scheme, he would have directed his steps towards
Acquetneck.   The Mooshassuc was not his first choice.   Had
he done so, as he had once intended, he would have found
greater resources of every kind.   The varied materials of the
colony might have been united in one town, for which they
were not too many.   It would have possessed greater breadth
and comprehensiveness than belonged either to Providence
or to Newport, and would have gained a wider audience from
the beginning.   The settlement at Mooshassuc would have
been later in date, and its history unlike what it is.*

When the unforeseen events suddenly befell him, Williams
had not, like Massachusetts, a charter, with a tolerably well
defined boundary, with full right of soil and jurisdiction.   He
was not unaware of the infirmity of his title.   In one of his
earliest letters to Governor Winthrop,† he speaks of his
occupancy as merely provisional —"until we hear further of
the King's pleasure concerning ourselves."   Their government was a mere agreement, "the inhabitants to pay 30s.
apiece as they came."   It was Williams's first intention to apply
to the government of England for a charter.   But he felt no
assurance that a charter would be granted, embodying his
political ideas, or that the people would be allowed to elect
their officers from among themselves.   To the Crown no application was made until 1644, and then only in union with
Newport.   During several years the Plantation suffered the
evils of a want of legal organization, and of security of title.
After Williams had built by the spring at Mooshassuc, it was
still legally competent for any other Englishman with a company of followers, to encamp on Fox's Hill and set up a rival
government with an authority as good as his own.   The

---

*When the place was first called " Providence," does not appear.
There is no vote to that effect to be found among the fragments of the
early records.

†Narragansett Club's ed., pp. 5, 6.

king might have confirmed the title of either, upon terms wholly subversive of their principles of government. It is probable that only the troubles of the times prevented this interference. Williams seems to have thought that an Indian title was a sufficient protection. He seems not to have been aware that as against the English government he and his company were only trespassers upon unoccupied lands of the Crown. Williams had no knowledge of English law, and did not consider that if any dispute arose over the title to the soil, the final decision would be given by the Privy Council or by the king's commissioners according to the rules of the common law, by which his proceedings were void *ab initio*. The despotic rule of Massachusetts had forced the settlers of Rhode Island into the undesirable position of giving the first exhibition of "Squatter Sovereignty" in the new world. It was a still greater misfortune of the new State, that the suddenness with which it was founded left no opportunity to settle the principles of its organization. The new home had not yet been purchased, and future relations at home and abroad were in a state of uncertainty. , The Planters at Mooshassuc were agreed upon but one principle, and that a negative one as to what the State should *not* do. They were agreed as to the foundation of a free commonwealth, but had given little attention to details. They did not clearly comprehend their relations with each other. Hence, at a very early day, the germs of many controversies began to develop themselves. Thus, in a letter to Governor Winthrop (of 1636 or 1637), Williams asks his opinion on "Whether I may not lawfully desire this of my neighbours, that as I freely subject myself to common consent, and shall not bring in any person into the town without their consent, so also that without my consent, no person be violently brought in and received?" Williams felt the highest respect for the character of Governor Winthrop and consulted him on the gravest matters. He would never have proposed any trivial or hypothetical question in their correspondence. It would seem that he had already submitted this question to the town meeting, and that the power of veto upon admissions of new freemen had been denied him. It would have given him the future control of the town. On the other hand, Harris and his associates always maintained and believed that Williams made his purchase from the Sachems, only as the agent of the whole body. The founder was to have no authority superior to that of one of his followers. In justice both to Williams and to Harris, these difficulties of the early planters should be remembered, and the ample opportunities for mistakes and misunderstandings which they afforded.*

All thoughts of homesteads and estates were delayed, by want even of an Indian title. So soon as he was able, in the earliest days of the Plantations, Williams sought an interview with the chief Sachems, and obtained from Canonicus and Miantonomi a gift, or at least a promise, of land sufficient for a town. This agreement was of unknown date and is not now extant. Judge Staples thought that it was merely verbal. Upon such an insecure foundation, nothing could be built. Canonicus was old,— his less trustworthy successor might retract his guaranty. Another negotiation was opened, in "the Second year of our Plantation," at which only Williams and the Indians were present. A memorandum was prepared — it was no deed. It was solemnly attested by the Sachems in the presence of Indian witnesses.† It is in these words : —

"At Nanhiggansic the 24th of the first month, commonly called March, in ye Second yeare of our Plantation, or planting, at Mooshausic or Providence.

"Memorandum, that we, Canonicus & Miantunomi, the two chief Sachems of Nanhiggansick, having two years since, sold unto Roger Williams, ye lands & meadows upon the two fresh rivers called Mooshausic & Wanasquetucket, doe now by these presents, establish & confirme ye bounds of those lands, from ye river & fields at Pautuckqut, ye great hill of Notquonchanet, on ye Northwest, & the town of Maushapauge on ye West.

"As also in consideration of the many kindnesses & services he hath continually done for us, both with our friends

---

*I have already described in Rider's Hist. Tract No. 15, the mode of planting and building the town, and need not repeat what was there said.

†R. I. Col. Records, Vol. I., pp. 18, 19, 26.

at Massachusetts, as also at Quinnichicutt, & Apaum or Plymouth, we do freely give unto him, all that land from these rivers, reaching to Pautuxet River, as also the grass & meadows upon yᵉ said Pautuxet River. In witness whereof we have hereunto set our hands."

Yᵉ Mark of ⟨⟩ Cannonicus.

Yᵉ Mark of Miantunnomi.

In the presence of

The Mark of ◯ Soldash.

The Mark of Assotemewit.

1639. Memorandum 3ᵈ Mo. 9 day. This was all again confirmed by Miantonomi; he acknowledged his act and hand, up the streams of Pawtuckqut, & Pawtuxet, without limits, we might have, for use of cattle.

Witness hereof   Roger Williams.*
Benedict Arnold.*

The first memorandum (it was no deed in a legal sense) was probably the work of Williams alone. The second memorandum, unlike the first, has no mention of the place of its execution, and has no Indian witness. Probably it received the assent of Miantonomi at one of his visits to Providence, and William Harris, who was in communication with Benedict Arnold (neither of them lovers of Indians), suggested the last clause which was the origin of such bitter controversy during the next forty years. Such was Williams's opinion as to its authorship.† The first memorandum was prepared without such legal advice as Williams might have obtained.

*They were the only two men in the Colony who understood the language of the Indians.

†See Williams's second letter to John Whipple, Rider's Hist. Tract No. 14, pp. 27, 29, 30, 31, 33, 34, 44.

He did not consult with William Harris, with whom his quarrel had not yet begun. Harris's ready and correct use of legal phraseolgy, suggests that he might have had the training of an attorney, or of an attorney's clerk. John Throckmorton* had been an officer of an English Municipal Corporation.† He had made large purchases of real property in Massachusetts and elsewhere, and must have known the proper terms of an ordinary purchase deed.‡ Governor Winslow of Plymouth, was a good friend to Williams, and knew at least the rudiments of English law. Any of these could have told him that his boundaries were vague, confused and almost certain to become the subjects of controversy,—that his grant had no "words of inheritance," and at Common Law gave him only a life estate. It does not seem to have occurred to him that a defect in such a title would be finally adjudicated, not between himself and the Sachems, in an Indian Council or in a Providence town meeting, but between two parties of Englishmen — between himself or his assignees on the one side, and some other Englishman setting up another Indian purchase or title by occupancy or possession on the other — and that the controversy would finally be determined by the king's courts, according to the rules of English law. A matter of such grave importance would have justified delay in order to send to England for appropriate forms of conveyance. But Williams had an obstinate will and an irritable temper, and was very impatient of opposition. As we shall see in several instances hereafter, so on this occasion, Williams, as was his wont, took counsel with no one, even where the rights of others were affected by his action.§ He ventured alone into the wilderness to the Indian stronghold at Narragansett, and secured such a title as his own unaided foresight permitted.

*At one time, Throckmorton was the owner of one-half of Prudence Island.

†See George Fox digged out, p. 13.

‡See Weeden's Social History of N. E., Vol. I., p. 109.

§See letter of Richard Scott, Appendix to Fox's " New England Firebrand quenched," " He must have the ordering of all their affairs, or else there would be no quiet agreement among them."

The first memorandum was vague and inconsistent in its description of the property conveyed. It seems to have been unsatisfactory to the associates of Williams. A long delay followed, and after two more years, the second memorandum, called a "confirmation," was obtained from Miantonomi, with the additional words, "up streams without limits, we might have, for the use of cattle." This "confirmation" which the cautious barbarian did not subscribe, was merely a certificate by Williams and Benedict Arnold, of what the Sachem had said in their presence.* Williams has left no account of his reasons for subscribing a document which he ever afterward so greatly disapproved. The second memorandum had no legal validity, was mere hearsay. But it was accepted at last by the purchasers, in despair of obtaining any thing else. The Planters—Williams among them—never reposed the same confidence in Miantonomi, as in the great Sachem Canonicus. It was deemed expedient to procure the confirmation of the heir to the Narragansett throne, as no one could be sure as to his future disposition. His prospect of long life seemed fair. No one anticipated his murder by the consent or order of the United Colonies, with the approval of the elders.† His renewed assent to his gift or grant was regarded by all parties as worth purchasing, as a security for the future. It was readily given, and as against the Indians, the title seemed to Williams to be complete. William Harris, with greater forecast than his neighbors, saw at once that the lands within the bounds of the Indian purchase were insufficient for an English plantation. Canonicus was willing to give a larger tract, but the inferior sachems in the neighborhood of Providence, made such a clamour that the gift was curtailed, as in the memorandum. Williams says expressly, "the sachems and I, were hurried (by yᵉ envie of some against myselfe) to those short bounds, by reason of yᵉ Indians then at Mashapog, Notakunhanet & Pawtucket, beyond whom the

---

*William Harris says that a deed was after drawn up in proper form, and was tendered to Williams, but that he refused to execute it.

†See Savage's Winthrop.

sachems could not then go," &c.* Harris undertook to supply the defect by the clause which gave occasion to so much wrath in the future. The words attracted but little attention at the time. It was claimed at a later day by the Proprietors, that they gave to Williams's grantees the entire fee simple of the town, from the west side of the Seekonk River to the Colony of Connecticut. We shall meet this clause again, — "up streams without limits," &c., the question whether the rights which it conveyed were corporeal or incorporeal.

As if these embarrassments were insufficient, the Indian grantors of Mooshassuc knew nothing of the English language, and had no written discourse of their own. There is little reason to believe that they understood their concession in the same sense in which it was received and paid for by the English settlers. The Indians were Socialists in theory and practice. All their land belonged to the nation or tribe, with only a temporary *user* by the individual members. To the end, they never comprehended or approved the exclusive and individual property everywhere asserted by the Englishman, and never ceased growling over its inconvenience to themselves.

But whatever doubts may have been suggested by the title to the soil, the material wants of the settlers for the time suspended all other topics. They had lived two years in those "filthy smoakie holes," the Narragansett wigwams, and the companions of Williams were eager to begin their work. They could do little until they had obtained an allotment of their homesteads. Williams had procured a title exclusively in himself and their first controversy with him was now to begin. Its discordant elements came to view in the earliest days of the town. This is Williams's account of its earliest political organization : —†

"The condition of myself, and those few families here planting with me, you know full well. We have no patent, nor doth the face of magistracy suit with our present condition.

*See Williams's second letter to John Whipple, Rider's Hist. Tract, p. 27.

†See Williams's letters, Narr. Club's ed., Vol. VI., p. 4; Williams to Winthrop, p. 4, 1637.

Hitherto, the masters of families have ordinarily met once a
fortnight & consulted about our common peace, watch &
plantings, by mutual consent have finished all matters with
speed & peace. Now of late, some young men, single persons,
of whom we have much need, being admitted to freedom of
inhabitation & promising to be subject to the orders made by
consent of the householders, are discontented with their estate, & seek the freedom of voting also, & equality," &c.

The first settlers had on some unknown day, restricted
the suffrage to married men, who were also heads of families
—a restriction far from welcome to the class, young and ener-
getic— but of little wealth, who are the majority in every
new Plantation. Their request was denied and they remained
in a state of discontent during nine years. They were then
enfranchised by a popular commotion which ended the voluntary association, or "town fellowship," and had well nigh
wrecked the Plantation itself. As to the number of these
young men at the time when Williams wrote to Winthrop,
we are not informed, but they must have been a considerable
proportion of the planters of those early days.

The founder and many of his associates had not much in
common. His purpose was threefold : first, to establish a
a free community in which the State should have no authority in matters of religious belief ; second, as akin to this, to
afford a refuge for fugitives who sought a like enjoyment of
the freedom of conscience ; third, the religious and moral
elevation of the Narragansetts. He was not ambitious of
civil office as the founder of a colony, or of landed wealth,
such as was the ambition of every one at home. His followers did not share his unselfish purposes. Their experience
of the abuse of power in Massachusetts had made them impatient of all authority whatsoever. With unyielding per-
tinacity, they watched over their own liberties, and provided
homesteads only for themselves. The majority manifested
little sympathy with Williams, except in his negative opinion
as to what the State should *not* do. No religious society was
organized until the autumn of 1638. Out of nearly sixty householders only twelve united with Williams in its formation.
During the whole of the seventeenth century, its members

were a small minority of the townsmen and numbered so few adherents that they met in the small dwellings of those days, and a meeting-house was not required until A. D. 1700. The Town Meeting would give no invitation to fugitives from religious intolerance, and set apart no tract or reservation for their benefit. All who came hither, came at their own risk, and upon their own responsibility.* The townsmen were not historical scholars, but they had seen enough of history enacted in old England to be assured that modern martyrs were not always the most agreeable tenants or neighbors, and that they often appear to greater advantage in chronicles and epitaphs than anywhere else.

The motives which urged most of the planters of Mooshassuck, seem to have been rather political than religious. They had come to Providence for religious liberty, but only a few of them showed much desire for an active exercise of its rights by setting up any religious assembly. Their chief anxiety was to escape from the despotism of Puritan elders, and their goverment was "only in civil things." With the Narragansetts, the settlers at Mooshassuc felt little sympathy. Their chief interest in their barbarous neighbors was pecuniary—in the trade in beaver-skins and in liquors so energetically denounced by Williams. Only Williams, and Benedict Arnold, the Indian interpreter and trader, understood their "barbarous rockie speech."† The excessive imports of wines and spirits, far beyond the consumption of the English settlers,—and all duly entered in the town records,—prove what was the chief staple of the Indian trade ‡ These fully justify Williams's censures of the practices of his fellow-townsmen and his forebodings of a bloody retribution. Not one of them gave him any aid in his mission or was an enthusiast in any like purpose.

With these diversities of character and objects, we may

*In the autumn of 1638, thirteen persons formed the Baptist Society. In 1637, there were fifty-four *householders* in Providence purchase. The exact number of the population is not known.

†See George Fox digged out, Narr. Club's ed., p. 465.

‡See Early Records of the Town of Providence, Vol. II., p. 22 and Index.

well believe that Williams and his associates did not readily agree in the ownership or disposal of the estate which had come into their hands. In order to see more distinctly their mutual relations, let us look at the events of the time. Mooshassuc had no charter. The people could not incorporate themselves or assume any of the powers of sovereignty. There were as yet no other towns capable of uniting in a legislature and of wielding for a time some part of the royal prerogative. No union with Newport was in view ; there was no prospect that there would be any. Great nations were little desirous of colonies of such microscopic dimensions. There was not even a town government. The settlers felt such a dislike for the *regime* of Massachusetts, that they would tolerate nothing but a voluntary association, or "town-fellowship." How then could Williams secure the great object of his life, and the planters the object of theirs? He wanted little for himself, but how could he secure the building up of a town by a people who could not bear heavy taxation, and who could hope for few wealthy emigrants? Disputes about such matters probably caused the long interval between the Sachems' "Memorandum" and Williams's "Initial deed."* There must have been a dispute at the outset of a grave character, that these homeless settlers denied themselves any fixed abodes until it was determined. There was first of all (as we have seen), the question of the authority of Williams to veto the admission of new inhabitants ; and then, what was the meaning of the "Initial deed"? But at length, finding that they could extract nothing else from him, the townsmen accepted the conveyance, such as it was, with all its uncertainties of meaning. Its boundaries are merely a reference to those in the Sachems' gift, with no explanations to make them clearer. Nothing can be inferred from the want of a seal, or witnesses, or of "words of inheritance." These were not in general use in Providence, until regular legal forms were introduced, in another generation. The deed of Williams to his associates was in these words : —

*From the 24th of March, 1637, to 8th of October, 1638.

"THE INITIAL DEED" FROM ROGER WILLIAMS OF THE LANDS PURCHASED OF CANONICUS AND MIANTONNOMI.

"Memorandum. That I, R. W., having formerly purchased of Canonicus and Miantonomi, this our situation or plantation of New Providence, viz. the two fresh rivers Wonas, and Moosh and the grounds and meadows thereupon, in consideration of £30 received from the inhabitants of said place, do freely & fully pass, grant and make over, equal right & power of enjoying and disposing the same grounds & lands unto my loving friends and neighbors S. W. WA. TJ. RC. J G, IT, WH WC TO FW. R. W. and E. H. and *such others* as the major part of us shall admit into the same fellowship of vote with us. As also I do freely make & pass over equal right & power of enjoying & disposing the said *land & ground*, reaching from the aforesaid rivers unto the great river Pawtuxet with the grass & meadow thereupon, which was so lately given & granted by the two aforesaid Sachems to me.

Witness my hand

R. W."

The original of the "Initial deed" is not extant. The recorded copy is without date.* It appears that the deed was delivered 1637. In another conveyance made for some unknown reason, on the eighth of the 9th month, 1638, Williams again grants the same lands to such others as the major part of us shall admit into the same "fellowship of vote with us."

Here began the great controversy of the Plantations. What did this mean? Who were the grantees? What their character and capacity? and what was their estate? They are mentioned only by their initials, as if individuality and personality were not regarded. Williams ascribes this singularity in his deed to haste and want of time—a strange reason, in a matter of such importance, and which was utterly denied by Harris. The consideration of £30 was an entire sum. Such

*Staples's Annals of Providence, pp. 31, 33.

as might be paid by a single corporate grantee, and not by single purchasers, in minute shares. The only succession described by the deed was not a personal succession to one and his heirs, but a corporate succession to a perpetual body, continued in being by the vote of the entire fellowship, which has *successors* but no *heirs*.* Williams conveys to "such others as the major part shall admit into the same fellowship of vote with us." These words describe the acts of a corporate body or guild, which could act by majorities (as mere tenants in common could not), and which could dispose of its estate only for the use of the whole corporation. If the whole of the "Initial" grantees were to hold merely equal undivided shares, as tenants in common, how could those who were afterwards admitted to the same "fellowship of vote" devest the estate already vested in the first grantees? A mere vote of a town meeting could not transfer vested estates from one freeholder to another. How was any reservation to be made for future sufferers for conscience' sake if all the proprietary lands had been already vested in private ownership? Williams, as he always maintained, undoubtedly believed that he had transferred his Indian purchase to an association to hold it in trust until a future town was ready to receive it.

In the "Initial deed," Williams only refers to the first "Memorandum" of the Sachems' purchase, without mention of the second, containing the clause "up streams without limits." If he had believed that any part of his grant was incorporeal or a mere right of pasturage, he would have done wisely to mention his belief in his memorandum. He would have thus saved himself from future censure and mortification. But he was not a lawyer. In his "Initial deed" he speaks of his whole purchase as consisting of "lands and grounds," and nowhere explains in any extant document that he was conveying an estate which was in any part incorporeal. He always insisted that the sum of £30 was received by him

---

*Harris says that the £30 was only the sum paid to Williams, but that the sum paid to extinguish the claims of the Indians made the entire cost to the townsmen £160.

as compensation for his labor and expense in visiting the
Sachems and in procuring the grant, and not for the purchase
of the land from him by the townsmen. The "Proprietors"
or "Purchasers" were to pay each thirty shillings for their
"homelots" six-acre lots and farming lands (100 acres
each) and for no more. He had no intention of parting with
the whole purchase, which had cost so much pains and labor
for the sole benefit of men who were chiefly strangers to
him, and to whom he was under no obligations, in order that
they might make dividends among themselves, as shareholders in a private company.

In this view of his conveyance to his associates, Williams
persisted during the remainder of his life. He lost no opportunity of proclaiming it. Only a few passages need to be
quoted, which sufficiently prove that Williams believed that
he had conveyed his purchase in trust to his followers as a
society and not as individuals.

I.   On the seventh of the 9th month, 1657, Williams executed a deed to James Ellis, of his lands at Whatcheer,
which he had received from the town.* He inserted in this
deed a recital of factsnot at all necessary to his conveyance,
but which he intended as a manifesto to be preserved in the
town book — a memorial of his original purpose. In it are
these words, "He parted with his whole purchase unto the
Township or Commonalty of the then inhabitants."†

II.   In the original agreement establishing the voluntary
association of the settlers at Providence, to which Williams
was a party, we read : ‡ "The *town* by five men shall give
every man a deed for all his lands lying within the bounds of
the Plantations, to hold it by, in after ages."§

III.   In his letter to John Whipple, 24th of August, 1669,¶
Williams insists that the disposal of the land should be by

*Early Records of Providence, Vol. III., pp. 110, 111, 112.

†See Staples's Annals, p. 37. Letter to John Whipple, Rider's Hist
Tract No. 14, p. 16.

‡Staples's Annals, p. 42.

§Fifth of 5th mo., 1640, R. I. Col. Records, Vol. I., p. 27, Sec. 1.

¶Rider's Hist. Tract No. 14, p. 38. MS. in the Library of the R. I.
Hist. Society.

the freeholders at large, in the town meeting. "Grant that
there have been discourses & agitacions many, about yᵉ lands
& purchases, yet is it not reasonable & righteous in all men's
eyes. Yᵗ since there are so many purchasers who ordinarily
doe not & others yᵗ will not come to yᵉ Towne Meeting, yet
their consent should be had, and yᵉ consent of yᵉ majorities
should determine yᵉ matters of their purchase, & oblige the
minor differing from them? I understand not yet of the
dammage of a farthing yᵗ any of you have sustained, or are
likely to do, from those whom you count your adversaries."
This passage relates to the claim of the Proprietaries to an
exclusive right to vote in the town meeting upon all matters
relating to the proprietary estate.*

IV. Williams is still more emphatic in his declarations
respecting the "Initial deed," in his "answer to the Declaration of William Harris against the Town of Providence,
seventeenth 9th mo., 1677, so called."†

"As to my selling them Pawtuxet & Providence It is not
true that I was such a fool as to sell either of them especially
as W. H. Saith, 'like an Halter in a market, who gives
most.' The truth in the holy presence of the Lord is this.
W. Harris (W. H.), pretending religion, worried me with
desires that I should admit him & others into fellowship with
my purchase. I yielded & agreed that the place should be
for such as destitute (especially for conscience' sake), & that
each person so admitted, should pay 30s. country pay, towards
a town stock, and myself have £30. towards my charges which
I have had, £28. in broken parcels in five years. Pawtuxet I
parted with, at a small addition to Providence (for then that
monstrous bound or business of "up streams without limits"
was not thought of). W. Harris & the first twelve of Providence were restless for Pawtuxet, & I parted with it upon the
same terms, viz. for the supply of the destitute, & I had a
loan of them (then dear), when these twelve men, (out of
pretence of conscience & my desire of peace) had gotten the

*This will be mentioned again.
†Rider's Hist. Tract No. 14.

power out of my hands, yet they still yielded to my grand desire of propagating a public interest, & confessed themselves but as feoffees for all the many scores who were received afterwards,—paid the 30*sh.* not to the purchasors so called, as Proprietors, but as feoffees for a *Town Stock:* & William ffield the builder of this house, & others, openly told the new comers that they must not think that they bought & sold the right to all the lands & meadows in common, & 100 acres presently, & power of voting, & all for 30*sh.* but that it went to a town & public use," &c.*

It is needless to multiply citations from Williams to prove his understanding of his deed to his associates. But they had other views of their own rights and interests, and would not abandon them without contest. They have left no diaries or letters, except a few by William Harris. It appears sufficiently from Williams's own writings that they had come to Providence with no clear understanding of their mutual relations.† Williams says in his "answer," "He" (*i. e.*, Wm. Harris) "chargeth Roger Williams for taking the land of Providence in his own name, which should have been taken in the name of those which came up with him." Whether this were a correct view of the matter or not, it is certain that many of the ablest of the planters of Mooshassuc entertained it. They were confronted at the outset with the questions whether this were to be an Indian mission under the direction of Williams or a town, and how far Williams's opinions were to be authoritative or decisive. They began with the debate as to whether the soil were individual property or corporate, like the land now held by the city at Field's Point, the Dexter Asylum, or Roger Williams Park. It was Williams's habit, as we shall see, to act upon his own opin-

*The house where Williams was then writing, was at that time the house of Thomas ffield. It was afterwards "fortified" and was the "garrison house" during Philip's War. It was the largest house in Providence. It stood upon the lot where the Providence Bank now stands, at a short distance eastward from the street. The last of the Field owners sold the property to Joseph Brown. Through his family it came to the Providence Bank.

†See also Rider's Hist. Tract No. 14, pp. 53, 55, 56 57.

ions or impulses without consulting others, however their
rights might be affected by what he did. So it was with respect to this vague and ineffective "Initial deed." But here
he had his opponents at a disadvantage. He alone had any
influence with the sachems, and the townsmen must take
such a deed as he chose to give them or lose the territory
altogether. No other person could obtain a grant of it.

They hesitated during several months. Harris says in his
"answer," or plea to his majesty's court, that "Williams's writing initials in his deed was a mere pretence of haste ; that
he promised a more formal deed, but that when one was drawn
& tendered to him he refused to sign it." At last the townsmen sullenly acquiesced,—accepted the "Initial deed,"—and
resólved to indemnify themselves in some way. They did so
effectually.

There was something to be said in their behalf. From the
hasty manner of the foundation there had been no definite
understanding of the views of both parties as there should
have been. They had all lost something,—the greater part of
their substance and all their prospects in Massachusetts.
They doubtless looked for some compensation for their sufferings beyond the thirty shillings' worth of wilderness land
which Williams had allowed to each of them. The "Initial
deed" created no express trust. This was only Williams's
inference. There were no means of enforcing the application to public purposes of money arising from the sale of
lots. Here, in the absence of any coercive judicial power,
was the weak point of Williams's whole machinery. The
creation and management of city property had been familiar in England for centuries. But Williams did not seek
advice from any quarter as to the proper mode of applying
real estate to specific objects. He had consented to a mere
government by arbitration, and he had no means of preventing the diversion of his grant to any purpose whatsoever. He
had required no covenants or conditions from his grantees,
and they, or Harris at least, soon perceived the weakness of
their obligations.

Their title was not such as they had expected or desired,
but as they could obtain no other, they went on under its

security to build and plant. There was no question at the time that the estates within their bounds were both permanent and corporeal.

That there was dissatisfaction at the first seems evident from the fact that the Pawtuxet "purchase" was contemporaneous with the "Initial deed." Williams has not left it a secret that the beginning of the town was not in harmony and peace. The grave question was left unsettled whether the new domain was to be the property of the whole society and of its political successors of the same "fellowship of vote," the few original settlers receiving only small allotments of homesteads and farms, or whether they and their heirs were to be tenants in common of the whole purchase, for their own private use. Williams seems to have been even alarmed at the dissatisfaction which he had created among his followers by the vague phraseology of his "Initial deed," for which he would substitute no other. There was a widespread uncertainity as to the future. New purchasers were arriving to partake of the freedom of Mooshassuc. These found the whole tract claimed by a few "purchasers," or "proprietors," who could at their pleasure exclude any one from the soil. These last were equally discontented with the small allotments which had been made to them. The separation between Proprietors and Freeholders at large began thus early. This is Williams's explanation* in his defence against William Harris : "I have always been blamed for being too mild, & the truth is Chase Brown [a misprint for Chad Brown], a wise & Godly soul, now with God, with myself, brought the murmuring after-comers & the first *monopolizing twelve* to a oneness by arbitration, chosen out of ourselves, & Pawtuxet was allowed (only for peace's sake) to the first twelve, and the twelve gave me a share, which I accepted, after the arbitration." Something must be done to allay the excitement, and Pawtuxet lands were the price of peace.†
By an agreement as informal as any of the preceding, and perhaps of uncertain date as to month and day, "the meadow ground" at Pawtuxet, bounding upon the fresh river upon

*Rider's Hist. Tract No. 14, p. 58.
†See Bartlett's R. I. Col. Records, Vol. I., pp. 19, 20, 21.

both sides, "is to be impropriated unto 13 persons being now incorporate with our Towne of Providence." The purchase money for Pawtuxet (£20) was to be paid to Roger Williams. Harris and the first twelve comers were thus in some measure consoled by the grant of large and valuable estates for the small homesteads which were their allotments under Williams's deed. Among the Pawtuxet men were those who retained the greatest sympathy with the civil and religious ideas of Boston, as they proved at no distant day. No new town was created. Like every thing else, this was left to the future. The bounds of the "Pawtuxet purchase" were so vague and unskillful that they furnished the material for a controversy which lasted more than seventy years. But they purchased a present peace and nothing more was expected. Had the far-seeing project of Williams been adopted, and had the Indian purchase been made a trust-fund, held by the town, there would have been, during two or three generations, some revenue; first, for highways and bridges and other works of immediate necessity which would have attracted immigration, — and afterwards for schools and other public institutions, without which free government was impracticable. The other alternative, which in the end was chosen, was the diversion of the whole estate to the profit of a private corporation, without regard to the interest of the commonwealth. Williams, like his followers, was borne away by enthusiasm for a rule by popular consent and arbitration. When it was too late he found that the unenlightened majority of his followers could act at their own pleasure. They were parties, witnesses and judges in the popular courts which they established.

The twelve grantees of Williams's "Initial deed" soon learned by experience that their rough and impracticable estate could only be managed by a society. During some years most of the new comers who had the means of purchasing property, were admitted into the "Town Fellowship" and became "purchasers," or "proprietors." Immigrants were not very many, and during several years the Proprietors were in fact the town. So long as this arrangement served their purpose, they readily agreed that the lands were conveyed to them as a society.

The "report of arbitrators at Providence," "containing proposals for a form of government,"* agrees that the disposing of the lands belonging to the " *Town* " of Providence shall be "in the whole inhabitants, by the choice of five men," "for general disposeall." But those who were not Proprietors were not yet voters, and it was not then foreseen that they would be. Some expenditures for surveys and for the care of the estate were needed at an early day. The Proprietors who constituted the "Town fellowship," soon formed a private society for the care of their estate and to determine whom they should admit into their number. Through the original defectiveness of the town records and the destruction of documents, in 1676, and in later times, the beginning of the Proprietors' association cannot now be ascertained, nor the circumstances of its origin. It was during many years zealous and adroit in its management of the town meeting and was not less so after the Proprietors had ceased to be a majority of the freemen and while enough of the estate remained to be a subject of attack or controversy.

There was little variety in the occupations of the members of the " Town fellowship." It was without skilled artizans, mechanics or professional men, and, save Williams, it had no man of liberal education. It had no coercive authority— had not even a constable, but was merely a voluntary association. It was subject from its earliest days to violent discontents and disturbances. The purchasers from Williams, the original twelve and their successors, insisted upon the sole enjoyment of the "fellowship of vote," in the town meeting. The landless younger portion of the society still claimed that they should not be excluded from the body politic, as we have seen that they claimed at the beginning.† No State or society lasts long before its members break into at least two parties, and Mooshassuc was no exception to the rule. There appeared at an early day the germs of two parties, which grew stronger as the town increased, and kept it in perpetual turmoil. Some were disappointed in what they found here, and some were captious and discontented. Some

*Bartlett's R. I. Records, Vol. I., Sec. 2, p. 28.
†Williams's letter to Winthrop, 1636-7.

had come from Massachusetts to escape its intolerance and
the arbitrary rule of its magistrates and elders. Beyond this,
which was but negative, they had but few positive opinions
in common. About twelve families sympathized with Williams in his religious opinions, but the majority kept aloof
from all associations of the kind. Some were noisy declaim-
ers, like Hugh Bewitt,—only in their element in a controversy which seemed the more welcome as it was the more
profitless,—and who seemed better fitted to receive toleration than to give it. Some were political agitators like Gregory Dexter, who had spent their lives in revolutionary
debates in England, and whose ideas concerning the foundations of civil authority and property were shadowy and indistinct. ᶜ Many of the small freeholders shared with Williams
in the belief that the lands purchased from the Narragansetts
were held by the Proprietors assembled in town meeting only
in trust for the whole body of the "freemen" admitted to
"inhabitancy." Against all these were the "Proprietors or
Purchasers," who claimed that the land was administered
only by the town meeting, for the sole use of those who had
paid for it and who had borne the burden of the settlement.
Some of these were among the most prominent citizens, and
men of no little ability. They saw that Williams's purchase
would one day be of far greater value, and desired to secure
for their children the benefit of their fathers' labor. They
contended that their purchase from Williams was their own
private estate. These parties were in full activity until the
Indian war, which brought an unexpected solution of much
of the difficulty. They were permanent, for they represented
interests of a permanent character. The feeling that they
were unjustly treated could not be allayed, while the less
wealthy freemen saw the most valuable purchases of woods
and waters restricted to the few, who could limit their own
numbers and apportion the domain among themselves.

The "agreement" subscribed by the "second comers," or
the "second set admitted," contains the terms of "fellowship"
—we can scarcely call it "citizenship"—in the voluntary
association at Mooshassuc.*

*See Bartlett's R. I. Col. Records, Vol. I., p. 14.

The precise time of the arrival of the party of "second comers," or the "second set admitted," is not known. It included Chad Brown, William and Benedict Arnold, John Field, William Wickenden and others, afterwards conspicuous in town and colony. This was the "agreement" of the "second comers:" "We, whose names are hereunder, desirous to inhabit in the Town of Providence, do promise to subject ourselves, in active & passive obedience, to all such orders or agreements as shall be made for public good of the body in an orderly way, by the major consent of the present inhabitants, *masters of families*, incorporated together in a town fellowship, and others whom they shall admit with them, only in civil things." The whole government was to be by consent and arbitration, and the right of voting was reserved to heads of families. All others admitted subscribed some similar writing or agreement. As immigrants arrived after 1638,— few indeed in numbers during the first years,— they were subjected to a strict examination by the town meeting. During several years this town meeting was composed of "Purchasers;" *i. e.*, holders of Proprietors' shares alone. Their scrutiny was rigorous. Little was left unknown as to the candidate— who he was, whence he came, and how much he brought with him. If he possessed sufficient means, few objections were interposed. Solvency has at all times held the same place in Rhode Island which Puritan orthodoxy once occupied in Massachusetts. If an aspirant to the "town fellowship" showed himself to be in no danger of becoming chargeable to the public, his future brethren charitably concluded that he was sufficiently orthodox to have his abode among them. After being admitted as "an inhabitant" he then applied to the Proprietors as a distinct association for leave to become a purchaser of a "Proprietor's right," or "share." To each person thus admitted, there was measured out by the "Proprietors' surveyors," one hundred acres of meadow or other land, a "six acre lot," or a "stated common lot," as near as might be to his homestead, and a "house lot," or "home share," of about six acres with a front of from sixty to eighty feet on the "Town streete," and extending backward to the swamp, where is now Hope Street. The proprietors' surveyors were directed to make their returns to the town meeting. As appurtenant to these grants, the new "proprietor" had also his fractional share in the purchase money arising from future sales of Proprietors' lands. He was not required by any law, deed, or custom to account for it to the town treasurer. The town meeting in due time confirmed the surveyors' return, and the vote was entered in the "Town booke." The survey and its confirmation were generally the sole evidences of the title. Few deeds were executed in Providence during the years of the first charter. Only one book was used for all public records. The meetings of the same persons as proprietors of the purchase and as freemen of the town were holden at the same time and place. They both had the same moderator and clerk and were in all respects but one body, save that in later days, when the owners of small freeholds had become voters, the Proprietors only were admitted to vote upon matters relating to the so-called "common lands." The proceedings of both bodies were entered indiscriminately in the "Town booke," and it is not always clear in which capacity an act was done.

The most conspicuous figures in this contentious little assembly were Roger Williams, William Harris and Thomas Olney. All of them were men of resolute will, and Harris and Olney had no little executive ability, in which Williams was especially wanting. Williams was at the head of the popular party and Olney and Harris were the leaders of the Proprietors. Olney found that the care of his religious society did not require so much of his attention as to prevent his transacting a large part of the business of the town in the town clerk's office and elsewhere. In that age politics were controlled by religious doctrines, which also colored all English radicalism. This did not then as now attack the great biblical institution of landed property, or even the English modification of it. Olney, who stood in the front rank of the political liberals of his day, was as firmly devoted to the landed interest in Providence as the staunchest churchman could have been. The lines which then divided political parties often coincided with those of religious sects. The Proprietors found it for their advantage that the chief orator of Providence, who was one of the heads of its only religious society, was wholly devoted to their interests.   Harris had equal influence over that increasing body of freemen, whose devotional spirit was their least conspicuous characteristic.   As time went on the Proprietors at large became weary of the contentions about private matters, which formed so large a share of public business.   Thus says Williams, 24th August, 1669, so called : "Grant that there have been discourses & agitations many, about ye lands and purchasers, yet is it not reasonable & righteous in all men's eyes, y^t since there are so many purchasers who ordinarily doe not & others that will not come to ye towne meeting, yet their consent should be had, & the consent of that majoritie should determine the matters of their purchase, & oblige the minor, differing from them."*   All such absentees were willing to leave their interests in the charge of Olney and Harris.   At a very early period the whole body of Proprietors become strongly organized, with able and sagacious representatives. These retained their leadership during life and handed it on to successors in a generation when the Proprietors were far less than the majority of the town.†

Other causes for the scanty attendance at the town meetings might be found.   In the early days of the town each householder was authorized to leave one man of his family at home on town meeting and training days, as a safeguard against Indians.   It was, as years went on, yet more difficult to procure a quorum in an assembly where all legislative, executive and judicial business was transacted by the same body as was also that of sales and exchange of lands. Special meetings could also be called on the requisition of any freeman who fancied that he had an affair of his own of sufficient importance to be inflicted upon his neighbors.

These rude political arrangements, with all their difficulties about boundary lines, majorities and special town meetings,

*Williams, as we have seen, always desired that the majority of the whole town meeting should decide upon sales of the town lands, and not the majority of the Proprietors alone, but he met with no success unto the end of his days.

†Early Records of Providence, Vol. II., p. 77.

answered the purpose of the settlers, so long as their numbers were but few. The written memorials of the first ten years of the town, are now, if they have not always been, very scanty and imperfect. They give a vague and indistinct view of its affairs. Yet there are indications that controversies were numerous and acrid even at that early day. The voluntary association, or "town fellowship," which endeavored to supply the place of government, but without coercive force, was but ill adapted to a community in which there was any considerable number of discontented people. It could only work harmoniously so long as the association of Proprietors was nearly coextensive with the town. The machine was in danger of going to pieces so soon as any considerable body of the inhabitants refused farther assent to a voluntary agreement, by which the townsmen were subjected to a close corporation of the first settlers. This occurred at an early period, but we have scanty information respecting the details.

The doctrine that civil government was nothing but a voluntary agreement, and that judicial authority was mere arbitration, did not tend to strengthen the State. Disorders began at an early day, and the town had no courts or magistrates which could repress them,— not even a constable. Young and landless men looked with envy upon "Proprietors" who were, or claimed to be, the sole owners of the unsold lands, and would not, if they could, prevent it, endure a monopoly of what seemed to be the gifts of nature. In England, at that day, when old opinions and institutions were becoming unsettled and were ready to fall, obscure religious fanatics began to hold forth doctrines about property, which all Christian denominations now repudiate and which belong only to the platform of atheism and anarchy. Some few, such as these, may have found their way to Providence, even at that early day. The smaller freeholders felt little scruple in helping themselves from the "common lands" whenever they needed timber, firewood or supplies, or food for their goats and swine, then a large part of their sustenance. Some of their acts were prompted by recklessness and malice,— such were the cutting down of trees bearing surveyor's landmarks. The Proprietors made, it seems, some feeble attempts

to restrain trespassers.   They only succeeded in irritating
and increasing the prevailing discontents.* Enmity between
classes went on and the acrimonious discussions which attended it.   Every thing was prepared for an onslaught upon
the voluntary association, so soon as a leader should appear.
He was not far to seek, for it was an age of revolutionary
ideas.   I have in a former paper reviewed at some length the
life and character of Samuel Gorton.   Little more needs to
be said at present than that he was possessed of more literary
education than any of the founders, save Williams.   He was
acquainted with Hebrew and with the Greek of the New
Testatment, and had a large acquaintance with the controversies then resounding upon every side.   He could suggest
doubts and difficulties respecting a great variety of religious
topics, although he had no well-defined system of his own.
In law and politics he understood his rights as an Englishman, better than did Williams or the Proprietors, or the
elders and magistrates of Massachusetts.   He knew that they
had no right to banish or expel him from their territory, and
against them he appears to have asserted no propositions
which he could not legally maintain.   He avowed monarchical
opinions of the old Biblical pattern and showed small respect
for any colonial government which had not legal authority,
meaning thereby, the sanction of the crown.   He deferred
to the authority of Massachusetts, for Massachusetts had a
charter and was administered in the king's name.   Gorton
well knew that in the view of Westminster Hall, the Proprietors of Mooshassuc were only squatters upon the king's
domain, who were bent upon closing it against all other
squatters but themselves.   He had never become a party to
their voluntary association, for he knew that it was merely
void.   He then, as at all other times, showed the courage of
his convictions and a wonderful talent for being disagreeable
to all whose belief and practices differed from his own.   He
was always ready to defy any authority which did not proceed
from the Crown.   He was no anarchist or bawler of what he
deemed a philosophical theory of property and rights, to be
put in force at the expense of other people.   If he told the

*All these things happened after the incorporation of the town, and
there is no reason to doubt that they were even more common before it.

Proprietors of Mooshassuc that their land monopoly was invalid,—that they had no rights by a private agreement of their
own to exclude the king's subjects from the king's domains,
he was not far from the truth. We know the character of his
doctrine only by its reflex effect upon Williams and Harris.
He was himself a landholder. He was no otherwise an atheist
or fomenter of sedition than as any one who denied the authority of Massachusetts elders would have been so represented by them, or than as one who claimed against them the
rights of a British subject under the common law.* Gorton
was no moneyless adventurer. His father had been a London merchant and a member of a guild, and his own wealth
(from the length and persistence of his legal controversies in
England) seems to have exceeded that of any of the Proprietors of Mooshassuc. Gorton *settled* in Providence sometime
before the 17th of November, 1641, and in January, 1642, he
purchased land at Pawtuxet. Soon after his arrival here he
began, as was his wont, to look about him for what was rotten
in the State, and there was no lack of those who were ready
to point it out to him. There were here young men discontented with their political disabilities, who had not found
here the equality which had been promised them, or which
they had promised to themselves. Others had found no satisfactory administration of justice. Gorton felt little respect
for the doctrinal peculiarities of either Williams or of his
opponents, and was quite their equal as a disputant. In a
society which numbered such leading men as Gregory Dexter, he was in no want of aid in an attack upon the rule of
the Proprietors. The outbreak was not sudden. The way
had been prepared for it by the discussions of the title of
Williams's grantees, and by the unfriendly relations of the
early freemen. The landless young men gave to Gorton ready
audience. The excitement spread among the small freeholders, and soon Williams was apprehensive that their whole

---

*His banishment from Massachusetts and from Plymouth is not to his
discredit. It was a proceeding unknown to the common law, and was
inflicted upon many whom we do not esteem the less on that account.
He was legally right in his contentions in Massachusetts and Plymouth.
His error was, in supposing that the elders and magistrates would respect any law but their own arbitrary will.

polity would be at an end. The topics of Gorton's discourses here are nowhere distinctly set forth. They were probably not unlike those which he had discussed elsewhere—the want of any legal foundation for political rule. He found here no religious establishment to be an object of attack, but the so-called "town fellowship" was even more objectionable than that of Newport or even than the Corporation of Massachusetts Bay. It is obvious that the old grievance of the proprietors' title to the whole territory and their virtual monopoly of power were at the bottom of all the trouble. There is no improbability in Winthrop's account of its beginning.*

Some attack had been made by the Proprietors upon those who allowed their swine to run at large upon the "common."† This was followed by forcible resistance and the uproar began. Winthrop was probably misinformed in his statement that "the parties came armed into the field," or that it was a contest into which any religious element at that time entered. The settlers did not care enough about ministers or denominations to fight either for them or against them. There was no need of armed resistance to the majority, or of a violent or bloody revolution. The town and its officers were but a voluntary association, and by the refusal of a minority to fulfill their agreement, the "town fellowship" was at an end. There was, as yet, no legislature and no coercive force in any quarter. Massachusetts and Connecticut did not interfere. They were content to look on and wait until the Rhode Island towns fell to pieces, and then, as at Pawtuxet and Newport, they could come in and gather up the fragments.

We know not how long the tumult lasted. The town records of that time have perished, even if they have not been voluntarily suppressed. Their affairs must have seemed well-nigh desperate when the leading Proprietors could have addressed their letter to the government of Massachusetts, asking its aid and protection.‡ By this address it appears

*Winthrop's Journal (Savage's ed.), Vol. II., p. 59. "The trouble in Providence began about a trespass of swine."

†Legislation upon this subject was frequent during the early years of the town.

‡The letter of William Field, William Harris and eleven others, is contained in second Vol. R. I. Hist. Coll., Appendix II., pp. 19 to 23.

that there were daily tumults and affrays, caused by the attempts of the freemen, under stress of necessity, as they averred, to obtain subsistence for themselves and their cattle from the wild lands, and by the endeavors of the Proprietors to arrest the depredators, followed by their forcible resistance, so that the peace of the town was at an end. Winthrop's Journal, by Savage, Vol. II., p. 59: "We told them that except they did subject themselves to some jurisdiction, either Plymouth or ours, we had no calling or warrant to interfere in their contentions." Winthrop speaks of the writers — the leading Proprietors — as the "weaker party," as they undoubtedly were. The dignified reply of Massachusetts taught to all parties a useful lesson by which they did not fail to profit in the near future.

This is the only public document of the controversy which is extant. It sufficiently exhibits the public alarm and excitement when the men who had fled from Massachusetts five years before, now besought its armed interference in their behalf.

In the midst of the panic, Williams did not lose his self-possession. Perhaps he was not wholly displeased at what seemed the overthrow of those who had thwarted his own cherished designs. He did not unite in the letter to Massachusetts. His only reference to the whole affair is in his private correspondence with Governor Winthrop (Narragansett Club's ed., Williams's letters, p. 141), Providence, March 8, 1646,* concerning Samuel Gorton. "Master Gorton having foully abused high & low at Aquidneck is now bewitching & bemadding poor Providence, both with his unclean & foul censures of all the ministers of this country (for which I myself have in Christ's name withstood him) & also denying all visible & external ordinances, in depth of familism, against which I have a little disputed & written, & shall (the Most High assenting) to death. Paul said of Asia —Inhabitants of Providence (almost all) suck in his poison as at first they did at Aquidneck. Some *few* & myself withstand his inhabitation & town privileges, without his confes-

*There seems to be some error in the date as printed. Gorton was in England from 1644 to 1648, prosecuting his suit against Massachusetts.

sion & reformation of his uncivill & inhuman practices at
Portsmouth. Yet the tide is too strong against us & I feare
(if the framer of hearts help not), it will force me to little
Patience, a little isle near to your Prudence," &c. It seems
that after civil broils had in some degree subsided, Gorton
resumed his polemics upon doctrinal matters and that from
their effect upon the general opinions of the townsmen, Williams's alarm began.   His sympathy with the men by whose
arbitrary will he had been banished, and who not long afterwards murdered Miantonomo, whipped Obadiah Holmes, the
Baptist, and hanged Quakers on Boston Common, will be
remarked by the reader of this extract. There is but little
other reference to Gorton in Williams's extant letters.* But
a natural termination came to this tumult also. The voluntary association was as powerless to give redress to the poor
freemen as to the proprietors. After some weeks or months
of disturbance it left both where they began. Gorton's lack
of executive ability and his restless disposition, did for the
Proprietors more than they could have done for themselves.
He saw a more inviting prospect in Pawtuxet and Warwick.
He speedily availed himself of it and withdrew Williams
came to the aid of his old opponents and assisted in restoring
order. (See his letter, p. 149, Narragansett Club's edition.)
The Proprietors who had converted his public trust into a
land speculation had looked on with dismay. They now took
heart again as they found that other parties were ready to
join them in an effective government. They saw that they
could not safely reject all the lessons which they had learned
in England and in Massachusetts. If they hoped to exist as
a community they must have a government.

This cloud passed over, but all parties saw that they must
modify their projects and make some concessions. The
Proprietors learned that their monopoly would avail them
little in a community where property had only the support of
a voluntary association. The dissentients saw that they could
not afford to give to Massachusetts any opportunity for in-
tervention, and all—that unless they put some restraint upon

*See also Winslow's "Hypocrisie Unmasked," p. 150, and Williams's
letter to the town of Providence, urging peace between the parties.

their tendency to disorder, England, then becoming Puritan,
would soon interfere in a fashion not agreeable to any, and
would probably introduce among them a class of fellow-
citizens and public officers whose notions of religious freedom
were very unlike their own. Some of the Proprietors, like
William Harris, were capable of thought upon political subjects. They saw the necessity of a legal foundation for their
establishment and of including some who were not of their
own body. It was evident, that in order to a harmonious town
government, the right of voting could not be vested in the
Proprietors or the house-holders alone. Heretofore, those
who had been "received as inhabitants," had, if they possessed the means, purchased "proprietor's rights," or "shares,"
and had become members of their society. The "second
comers," before mentioned, had brought some property with
them. They had accepted the situation as they found it,—
were zealous supporters of Harris and Olney, and gave little
aid to Williams in maintaining his theory that the Indian
purchase was to be "town stock." Some provision must be
made for the "young men of whom we have much need,"
mentioned by Williams, who were from time to time arriving
in yet larger numbers and who had but little to invest in
lands. The Proprietors were divided in opinion. The followers of Thomas Olney opposed all concessions, but they were
overruled by the more enlightened forecast of William Harris (See Williams's second letter to John Whipple, in Rider's
Tract No. 14). The dispute ended by the creation of a new
class of citizens who might become voters, with lower qualifications, which should be within the reach of all reputable
citizens.

"The 9th of the 11th month, 1645 (January 19, 1645-6).
We whose names are hereafter subscribed, having obtained
a *free* grant of twenty-five acres of land apiece with right of
commoning according to the said proportion of land from the
free inhabitants of the Town of Providence, do thankfully
accept of the same, & do hereby promise to yield active &
passive obedience to the authority of (King & Parliament)
established in this Colony, according to our charter, and to
all such wholesome laws & orders that are or shall be made
by the major consent of this Town of Providence, as also not

to claim any right to the purchase of the said Plantations nor any privilege of vote in the town affairs, until we shall be received as freemen of the said town of Providence."* This "agreement" was drawn up after the granting of the first (called the Earl of Warwick's) charter, but before any government had been organized under it. Many signatures of different dates are appended to the "Quarter-rights men's" agreement. They might be admitted to vote, but not to a *full* right of common. It was not intended to create a permanent class, but only to quiet a present trouble; and it accomplished its purpose. The effects of Gorton's agitation in overthrowing the voluntary association or "town fellowship" were permanent and beneficial. But his old enemies never forgave him for what he had done towards their downfall and carefully treasured up their wrath.

When the hubbub in Providence was quieted it was not easy to induce the other plantations to agree to a union with so turbulent a town. The disorders of Providence furnished to the men of Pawtuxet one of the chief pretexts for their secession to Massachusetts. Their cause of dissatisfaction had been at first only a question of land titles or boundaries. But in September, 1642, some of the Pawtuxet people seceded to the jurisdiction of Massachusetts. The town was brought into a speedy contest with its old enemies at Boston. Only a specimen need be given of the inconveniences which her dissentions brought upon Providence, during many disastrous years. Thus, so late as November 14, 1655. Town Meeting.† "Mr. R. Williams, Moderator." Ordered that the gathering of the rate at Pawtuxet be suspended until a letter be sent to the Massachusetts. "Town Meeting Records April 27, 29, 1656. At a Quarter Court, Mr. Roger Williams, Moderator * * it is ordered upon receipt of a letter

---

*A "right of common" is an incorporeal right of pasturage or other easement or profit in the land of another person or of the town. What the people of Providence called the "common" or the "common land" was the soil itself of which the Proprietors claimed to be tenants in common. It was not a "common" in any legal sense, but only unenclosed and unimproved land claimed by the Proprietors.

†Early Records of Providence, Vol. II., pp. 90, 93.

from the Governor of the Bay, that a man be sent thither to
treat about the business of Pawtuxet." Thomas Olney was
the commissioner. Mooshassuc was forced to submit to the
commands of Massachusetts to her great injury and loss.
During several years she derived no revenue from her most
populous dependency. The secession of Pawtuxet lasted
until 1658. The planters there had then discovered that
their gain by absorption into the larger province would be
but small. They grew weary of the contemptuous patronage
of Massachusetts and of their inferior position in a colony
from which they had hoped for greater freedom and security.
Massachusetts was willing to let them go and troubled them
no more. A like dissatisfaction prevailed in Newport even
after the Earl of Warwick's charter, and led to equally disastrous results in the secession of Coddington. The laws of
Newport were not unlike those of Providence, but she was
more vigorous in their execution. She made no boast of
being a voluntary association, but submitted to it only as a
necessity. The people of Newport were never in cordial
sympathy with those of Providence in relation to many subjects pertaining to religion and learning and social life.
They readily listened to emissaries from Plymouth who urged
their separation from turbulent Providence and a union with
their more orderly neighbors of Plymouth. These things belong to the history of the colony—not of the town, but they
require notice as part of the evil results of the attempts in
Providence to live without law and to govern without a government. After they had regained the control of the town
meeting the Proprietors were supported by all parties in
their endeavors to effect a union with the other towns. Warwick was not reluctant, but the people were few. It was not
easy to induce the people of Newport to join in an application for a colonial charter. The founders of Newport counted
among themselves some who had been high in social station in
Boston, and they did not hesitate to give utterance to their
opinions about Mooshassuc. Some years passed before anything could be accomplished, but the obstacles were at last
overcome. Gorton says (and he is generally accurate in his
statements) that the Newport men were disturbed by the

name of the new colony.   It was the colony of Providence
Plantations.   Newport feared that the younger, but more
numerous and wealthy, town was to become subordinate to
the older, but smaller and poorer and more disorderly Providence.   Newport assented at last, and a charter was obtained
in 1644.   But the reluctance of the islanders was so persist-
ent, that no organization could be effected until 1647.   Some
of the adherents of the voluntary association in Providence
had learned little by experience, and could not be induced to
abandon the "town fellowship," even for greater security of
title, until 1649—the year of the incorporation of the town
of Providence.   It was now to have a common seal and a
constable's staff.   These ancient signs of authority added
something to the force of government.*   More important was
the legislative permission to make penal enactments at their
pleasure.   The Proprietors readily seized the opportunity
thus given for the protection of their own estate.   After the
penalties enacted by the Proprietors against depredators upon
the "commons," the other voters were not the cause of much
apprehension.   The "Quarter-rights men" were uneducated,
of humble means, and unable to offer any effectual resistance to the organized body of Proprietors led by Olney and
Harris.   But the distinction of classes among the voters out-
lasted the first generation.   Their dissentions in the town
meeting and the town street from time to time broke forth
with a violence which (from Williams's allusions), we may
believe, did not always end in words.   It mattered not how
the young men voted upon ordinary matters, so long as they
had no votes upon questions relating to the Proprietary
estate.   Soon every thing went on as before.   The position
of the Proprietors was rather strengthened than otherwise,
by the enlargement of the constituency.   The "young men"
of Williams's letter found their "privileges" not wholly a
gain.   On the "1st 2d day in June, 1656," it was "ordered
that all inhabitants, though not as yet accounted freemen in
this towne, yet shall be liable to be chosen to doe service in

*Early Records of Providence, Vol. II., pp. x., 112, 113, 114.   27, 2d
Mo., 1649.   "Our constable is to have a staff whereby he is to be known
to have the authority of a town's constable."

this towne;"* *i. e.*, in mending roads and the like hard work, although not voters — a species of impressment after the fashion of the time.

The number of citizens was somewhat increased by the sales of the property of individual proprietors, as they found their private estates inconvenient, or as they died or left the colony. Thus, within a few years, there were three distinct classes of voters, who had little sympathy with each other — the Proprietors, the "Quarter-rights men," and the small freeholders at large. These were social distinctions as well as differences in estates. The Proprietors soon perceived that they had nothing to fear from the small freeholders. At a town meeting, May 15, 1658, which was under the control of their own body, for Thomas Olney was elected Moderator, it was "ordered that *all* those that enjoy *lands* in the jurisdiction of this town are freemen."† The social influence and *prestige* and such education as could be found were with the Proprietors, the first owners of the soil. The new freeholders were men of small estates, who had been admitted to residence and to purchases by the consent (the charity as they deemed it) of the proprietary class. Few of them were heard in the town meeting or proposed any of its votes.‡

As times went on, the Proprietors ceased to be unanimous. A minority of them supported the opinions of Williams. But the Proprietors on the other hand could always control the votes of a sufficient number of the small freeholders. In the town meetings none but Proprietors could vote upon any matter touching the proprietary estate. A troublesome freeholder could be quieted by a sale of land upon easy terms or for a nominal consideration, and thus the Proprietors were. enabled, during many years, to maintain their authority unimpaired.

The rule of the Proprietors had become so well established after Gorton's excitement, — perhaps in consequence of it,— that they felt no apprehensions, and went on to develop

*Early Records of Providence, Vol. II., p. 94.

†Early Records of Providence, Vol. II., p. 112.

‡During many years the towns fixed the qualifications of their own voters.

their institutions in their own way. However, some among them may have dreamed of an ideal liberty the world had as yet never seen, and of a rule by merely amicable agreement, yet the founders could not escape from the traditions and the rivalries of their own race and country. Landed property had been for centuries the ambition of the Englishman. It was then, as it has been ever since, the only possession which has afforded permanent personal and family distinction. The London merchant accumulated the profits of Fleet Street and the Strand that he might purchase the manors of worn-out feudal families and found a new peerage for himself and for his heirs. The serjeant hoarded his fees from the strifes of Westminster Hall for a like decoration of the chancellorship or chief-justiceship which was in prospect before him. A like ambition pervaded all the prosperous classes in England — soldiers or civilians. The same could not be done in an American colony, but everywhere, in the days when moneyed wealth had not reached its modern development, landed estates were the foundation of social rank and influence. The English ideal was perhaps most completely realized in the royal province of New York. But it was recognized and respected even in the humble beginnings of the plantations at Mooshassuc. Its founders availed themselves of such means as were at their command, and the landed polity which they founded lasted, with few changes, during nearly two hundred years. They were not consciously founders, but their scheme of government developed itself spontaneously out of existing facts. It was not established by law or charter and was copied from nothing which the townsmen had seen in England or in Massachusetts. It was not an ascendency of great landholders, for there were none; nor was it a despotic rule of magistrates and elders. All these they had left behind. When the colony was first organized,* it styled its polity "a democracie;" "that is to say, a Government held by ye free and voluntary consent of all, or ye greater part of y^e *free* inhabitants." This word "Democracie" has served many uses, some of them very unlike those of the present day. In Athens, men talked about democracy

*Vol. I. Bartlett's Colonial Records, 1647, May 19–21.

in a city state, one-half of whose inhabitants were slaves. South Carolina might have done the same. They meant by it an equality of political rights only among the members of the free or ruling classes who were within the pale of the Constitution and members of its guild or corporation, whatever the condition of those who were without it — the servile element — might be. If the dominant class were graded with permanent ranks, titles, guilds, professional, mercantile and literary, it was an aristocracy. But if the ruling class had no legal titles or distinctions, however wide might be the distinction of social rank, personal inequality did not prevent its being styled a democracy even though the laboring classes were slaves. The third generation of the landed democracy of Rhode Island offered little opposition to the establishment of slavery so soon as the people could afford it, as the first generation had sanctioned the distinction of the Proprietors and the Quarter-rights men.

It was not easy to weld so many dissimilar materials into one tenacious mass. Men who had lived thirteen years in a voluntary association with the theory that goverment was only a mere agreement, binding only upon those who had subscribed it, were not easily induced to submit even in "civil things" to a coercive jurisdiction, though authenticated by a "common seal" and "a constable's staff." Obstinate old habits were not easily overcome. Few seem to have given much thought to their new relations with each other or with their neighbor colonies or with their associated towns.

They were more anxious to conceal their proceedings from the government of England than to enquire how far they were entitled to her protection or subject to her control. There was little unity of religious opinion which might have given cohesion to jarring political elements. Massachusetts had gained this element of strength by excluding dissenters. The Baptists, the first society organized here by Williams, were not the majority of Providence. They numbered only thirteen families in a community of over fifty householders, and soon there was a secession even among them. The religious disputes among the townsmen, and which here as elsewhere displayed a rancour now unknown, added bitterness to political controversy.* Thomas Olney, Sen., was one of the successors of Williams in his small society. William Harris was one of the seceders. Satisfied with that brief experience, he united with no other congregation to the end of his days. These were the two leaders of the Proprietors. Unity in secular interests superseded all religious differences between them. Olney apparently influenced the more religious, and Harris the secular, element in politics. They were both able men and conducted the affairs of the Proprietors with vigor and success. Williams rarely suffered his personal resentments to grow cool. During many years when he had occasion to speak of Chad Brown, it was always with kindly remembrance, gratitude and respect. For Thomas Olney, his successor, he has no words of pleasant recollection. Where he has need to speak of him it is with the mere mention of his name. The first Thomas Olney, an elder in Williams's congregation, was a man of courage and tenacity of purpose. By his executive ability as clerk of the town and of the Proprietors he continued to the end of his days a leader in the affairs of both. Together, Olney and Harris were more than a match for Williams, Dexter, and their supporters.

The community at Mooshassuc had little to distract its attention from its one great topic of debate. It was far away from England — heard little of what was going on there, and that little long after the event. With Massachusetts their intercourse and correspondence were infrequent. Their chief anxiety was whether the "Bay people" intended to seize and annex their territory. They had no great political questions of their own. Religious topics — the great political topics of the 17th century — were, by general consent, excluded from the town meeting. They had ample

*See Backus's History of the Baptists, Vol. III., p. 217. "The unruly passions of some among them (*i. e.*, the Baptist Society in Providence), with other things, caused such scruples in Williams's mind in about four months that he refrained from administering or partaking of special ordinances in any church ever after as long as he lived; though he would preach the gospel and join in social worship with those who agreed with him, all his days."

See also Geo. Fox's A New England Firebrand quenched, pp. 63-68, 69, 127.

leisure to reiterate what had been said often enough in the
"towne streete" and at the town mill without changing the
opinion of any voter as to his own rights or those of the
Proprietors.

The "landed democracy" proceeded in their own time and
way. Even after the purchase of Mooshassuc their position
was still insecure. The eagerness of Massachusetts to acquire
the territory around Narragansett Bay, was unabated during
twenty years. The principles of Rhode Island were gaining
some converts in Massachusetts and Plymouth and inspired
anxiety and alarm among the magistrates and elders. What
could not be done by force might be effected by emigration.*
What its charter would not permit might be accomplished by
a few scores of emigrants. These, becoming purchasers, might .
subvert the institutions of Providence and set up those of
the "Bay people" in their stead. Some security must be
provided and the Proprietors in town meeting had done it
effectually. "1637. 16 die 4th mo." (as soon as a treasurer
had been provided "for expending the town's stock"), 2d year
of the Plantation.† "Item that none sell his field or his lot
granted in our liberties to any person but an inhabitant,
without consent of the town." [It then consisted chiefly of
Proprietors.] This restriction was needed, the householders
being as yet but few, that the control of the town might not
fall into the hands of new comers hostile to the opinions of
the founders. But in effect during two generations it gave
to the Proprietors alone the power to determine who should
be the future voters. In another subject of their legislation
their wisdom is less conspicuous. They were none of them

---

*The right of voting was then (during the first charter government of
Massachusetts) restricted to such freeholders as were "church members,"
who very soon became a small minority of the people. The secular character of the institutions of Rhode Island were a continual incitement to
the dissenters of Massachusetts.

†No originality was required in inventing contrivances for this purpose.
The same means which had been used by the towns of Massachusetts in
order to prevent any but Puritans taking up their abode in them were
equally efficacious in Rhode Island in excluding Puritans themselves.
See Adams's Three Episodes of Massachusetts History, Vol. II., p. 647.
Private persons were not permitted to sell their lands without the consent of the town.

merchants and did not desire that their children should ever be. The Proprietors of Mooshassuc had the courage of their convictions. From the first they showed no hesitation in adopting measures which would prevent or delay the rise of a commercial town in which their own association might become insignificant or might vanish away. It was right that the town meeting should prevent trespasses upon the home lots which it had granted, and reckless waste of timber.*

Such as these were their earliest regulations: *c. g.*†

"It is *agreed* that two men should be deputed to view the timber on the common and such as have occasion to use timber should repair unto them for their advice and counsel to fell timber fit for their use, between the shares granted and mile end cove."‡

"That from the sea or river in the West end of the Town unto the Swamp in the east side of the fields that no person shall fell any wood or timber before any particular man's shares end" (*i. e.*, on this side of the "swamp," now Hope Street). "Item. That any timber felled by any person, lying on the ground above one year after the felling, shall be at the Towne's disposeing, beginning at the twenty third *die* of the month above written."§ This is the earliest police regulation of the town now extant and was a reasonable restraint upon mere waste of timber and trespasses upon property, such as are common in all new countries. But as times went on, the agricultural Proprietors had become firmly established

---

*Adams's Three Episodes of Massachusetts History, p. 658. A. D. 1646. There were similar laws in many Massachusetts towns against exporting timber.

†Vol. I. Bartlett's Colonial Records of Rhode Island, p. 5. This was the style of the enactments of the " town fellowship "—"agreed."

‡There were large intervals between the shares then allotted and the water side at the south end of the town. It was built up at first only on the east side of the river which "was at the west end" of it. The home lots at the south end were not yet sold, in February, 1637–8, or even allotted. They were too remote from the centre.

§There were regulations for the same purpose — the preservation of timber — and nearly in the same words in many of the Massachusetts towns, from which these may have been transcribed. See Weeden's Social and Economical History, Vol. I., p. 109.

as the chief men of their respective neighborhoods, and such
they intended to remain. They gave no invitation to merchants such as they had known in Boston and Salem, whose
wealth would eclipse their own, and who might subvert their
religious liberties, which in those days found little favor with
the prosperous classes anywhere. After a few years the
town meeting at the dictation of the Proprietors began to
use the prohibition to fell timber trees as a restraint upon
shipbuilding and commerce.* Thus, "27th 11th mo. 1650. At
a Quarter Court, *Ordered* [this was the style of the newly
incorporated town meeting] that no person whatsoever,
whether townsman or other shall carry or cause to be carried
either directly or indirectly off the common, any fencing
stuff, botts, pipestaves, clapboards, shingles, pitchlights or
any other sort of building timber out of this Plantation without leave from the town, and if any be found so doing, he
or they shall forfeit to the Town for every tun of fencing
timber or other building timber, after the rate of 10 shillings
per tun, for every hundred of clapboards 10 shillings, for
every hundred of shingles after the rate of 2s. 6d., for every
hundred weight of pitchwood after the rate of 3s."†

This order of the town included Proprietors as well as
all others. As it did not answer the purpose of the agricultural Proprietors that the place should become a mart of
trade, they withheld from sale one of its chief staples. There
was no lack of timber, the whole country was a great forest
with only occasional openings of meadow land. Such enactments from time to time renewed, effectually prevented
trade with the West Indies and the Spanish Main, for which
timber, planks and barrel staves were prime necessities. The
least danger of the town was that of a want of fuel or building material. Yet the Proprietors reserved to themselves
the power to consent to its use as an article of commerce.
They very sparingly (if at all) granted the permission even
to their own members. They were successful in their narrow policy. The town was not inferior in resources to any

---

*Early Records of Providence, Vol. II., pp. 54, 57, 61.

†Early Records of Providence, Vol. II., pp. 54, 61. See also the order
of the town meeting, 27th 11th mo., 1651.

of the seacoast towns of New England. But through this restrictive legislation it had no fisheries, such as gained the earliest wealth of Massachusetts. Nor was there any shipping in the bay, save the vessels of other colonies, until the closing years of the 17th century. This may serve as a specimen of the proprietary zeal for the public interest. They were not less vigilant in protecting their own. The legislature in the charter of incorporation had authorized the town to enact penal laws at its own discretion. The Proprietors availed themselves of the opportunity for securing their own estate. They established fines, for those days severe, the burden of which fell upon the smaller freeholders. Such were the penalties for felling timber, for allowing swine and goats to run at large in the commons, and later for cutting the thatch beds at the mouth of the Wonasquatucket. An act of this sort upon the land of a private freeholder was but a trespass, the subject of a civil action. Done against the estate of the Proprietors it became a criminal offence and could be visited by the full power of the law — such as it was, in those days. The proprietary rule was now so well established that there was no fear of resistance even to an enactment like this : "7th 6th mo. 1650.* Ordered that a rate be levied upon the estates of *men* only, excepting lands that lie in common, and that the Town Council shall rate the same."† Thus the Proprietors secured exemption from taxes for all but their individual estates, notwithstanding their claim of the "common lands" as their own private property and their receiving for their own use the proceeds of the sales. We might believe this to have been an act of surprising boldness and unwisdom had it not been quietly endured by the freeholders until the end of the 17th century. Precisely how this exemption was borne we cannot ascertain from the town records. It was silently dropped when the Proprietary estate was much diminished. The same men who contended against Williams that their purchase from him was their individual property,

*Early Records of Providence, Vol. II., p. 50.

†From the use of this word *men*, it was some years later argued that *women* were exempt from taxation, and the claim was in part, during several years allowed.

now exempted it from public burdens as if it had been as he asserted,— a " town stock." The small freeholders could not resist the Proprietors. The information doubtless spread through the neighbor colonies that the inferior freemen in Providence bore an undue share of the public burdens, both of town and colony rates, and may, in part, account for the small number of those who sought to avail themselves of the freedom of the plantations.

Before many years, other equally singular notions about rights to real property became current among these un-learned legislators. Some of the Proprietors were not exempt from them, and were ready to enforce them upon those of their own brethren for whom they felt but little regard. There were no charges against Joshua Verin of being in any default in payment of taxes upon his private estate (his pro-prietary lands were not taxable), yet many of the townsmen were of opinion that his proprietary share might be forfeited by mere non-residence. He had left the colony after he had been censured for violating the liberty of conscience. From Salem he addressed the following letter to the townsmen, which was read at the town's Quarter-day meeting, April 27, 1651 : —

"Gentlemen & Countrymen of the Town of Providence : This is to certify you that I look upon my purchase of the Town of Providence, to be my lawful right. In my travel I have enquired and do find it recoverable according to law, for my coming away could not disinherit me.* Some of you can-not but recollect that we six which came first, should have the first convenience. As it was put in practice by our house lots & second by the meadows in Wonasquatucket River. And then those that were admitted by us, into the purchase, to have the next which were about ; but it is contrary to law,

*Weeden's Social and Economical History of New England, Vol. I., p. 270. In the earliest settled towns of Massachusetts it was not an un-common condition of the sales to the first grantees, that the lands should be forfeited if certain improvements were not made within a definite time. But such cases were not like that of Verin. He had been in pos-session by himself or by his agents during more than ten years—had built for himself a house. And it is not charged against him that his taxes were in arrears.

reason & equity, for to dispose of my part without consent. Therefore, deal not worse with me, than with the Indians, for we made conscience of purchasing it of them, and hazarded our lives. Therefore we need not, nor any of us ought to be denied of our purchase. So, hoping you will take it into serious consideration and to give me reasonable satisfaction. I rest, yours in the way of right and equity,

JOSHUA VERIN."

From Salem, the 21st November, 1650.

Men of understanding could not fail to see the disastrous consequences to the town (and to themselves also), of such a precedent as this. Who of them could foretell what might be done by a popular majority, if he himself should become unpopular in his turn? Forfeitures and confiscation were familiar in old England in that age, and this might be the beginning of the like practices here. It required the influence of William Harris, Thomas Olney, Epenetus Olney, and later on of John Whipple, to prevent the appropriation of Verin's estate by the town meeting.*

The curt answer of Gregory Dexter, the town clerk, shows that some proceedings had been commenced.† "The Town of Providence having received, read & considered yours dated the 21st November 1650, have ordered me to signify unto you, that if *you* shall come into court, & prove your right, they will do you justice." per me

GREGORY DEXTER, Town Clerk.

In this case the townsmen would have adjudicated a claim in which they were themselves plaintiffs. Gregory Dexter was one of the radical leaders of his times, and probably a promoter of the suit against Verin. When the Proprietors recovered their old ascendency they dropped Dexter from the clerkship, a place of great influence and profit for those days.

*See Bartlett's Colonial Records of Rhode Island, Vol. I., p. 17. Verin's letter contains some historical details concerning the plantation which are not elsewhere preserved.

†Early Records of Providence, Vol. II., pp. 55, 56.

John Whipple came to Providence from Dorchester, Mass., in 1659. He brought with him a larger property than was commonly possessed by the immigrants of that day. He was received as an inhabitant of the town, purchased a Proprietors' share,* and soon became a leading citizen and a zealous supporter of Harris and Olney. [Williams's second letter to Whipple, Rider's Tract No. 14.] Williams says that he was a constant speaker in town meetings (p. 42), and evidently regarded him as one of his chief opponents. He was licensed to keep an inn, and during many years kept the principal one in Providence in what is now "Constitution Hill." He was a man of ability and influence and his inn became the political centre of the town. It seems probable that Williams addressed his letters to Whipple, that they might become more widely known in what was then the chief club-house of the village. He died May 16, 1685.

Before many years the town meeting began to use the privileges which it had granted to the "twenty-five acre men," as a means of correction and discipline. Thus, "October 27, 1659. Thomas Olney, Senʳ. Moderator. * * Forasmuch as there hath been a Complaint made by some of the inhabitants, unto this Court against John Clawson for *making use* of the Common, it is therefore ordered by this present court, that the Deputies or Deputy of the Towne shall forthwith forewarne the said John Clawson to forbear in any wise to make use of *any* of the Common."† It does not appear what was the "head and front" of John Clawson's "offending." His name appears in the list of the "twenty-five acre men." He had probably not rightly estimated the extent of his privileges and made an excessive and indiscreet use of them. He was therefore wholly deprived of them and was thenceforth to draw no firewood or other household stores from the common land. This forfeiture of his rights was *ex post facto* and illegal, but such slight technical difficulties were of little account before the popular and unlettered judges of those days. By what right they could deprive one of their co-tenants of his due proportion of common is

---

*Early Records of Providence, Vol. II., p. 117, July 27, 1659.
†Early Records of Providence, Vol. II., p. 126.

not now apparent. But they did it notwithstanding.* For us, who have but lately celebrated the centennial of a constitution well provided with restraints upon the violation of contracts and the appropriation of private property to public uses, it is difficult to keep in our recollection while reading our early records, that during an hundred and fifty years there was no check upon the absolute power of a colonial assembly, except the uncertain and capricious interposition of a royal veto. In Rhode Island, even this security was wanting. We may meet with acts of its wholly secular legislation, quite as despotic as any of those of which its founders had complained under the rule of Massachusetts and its elders, or in old England under the monarchy of Charles the First.

These two cases of Verin and Clawson are sufficient examples of the acts legislative and judicial, which were characteristic of the first *régime* in the plantations. They were attended by arrangements equally unsafe for the management and transfer of real property. Every thing in the early records shows the handiwork of men without experience in such duties. Their early enactment, that no purchaser should sell his lot without leave of the town meeting, was justified by the danger that in a small community, unprotected by a charter from the Crown, a sufficient number of freeholds might be acquired to give to a hostile colony the political control of the town. But this was the only security provided by law. The transfers of property were without formality or precision. No *deed* was thought *necessary* until the days of the second charter. As the "stated common lots" were but small (of some ten or twelve acres each), and were widely separated, they did not add much to the wealth of the settlers. From the constant petitions to exchange or to relay them, it might be inferred that they were often a hindrance to the culture of the soil.†

*This proceeding against John Clawson seems very much like a specimen of Massachusetts justice, as dispensed by the magistrates and elders. They were ready to make their law for the occasion, without much enquiry whether it were *ex post facto* or otherwise, provided that it suited their own notions of what the case required.

†For examples see Early Records of Providence, Vol. II., p. 55. Roger Williams asked for liberty to exchange his lands, Sept. 30, 1667.

The "Land Records" of Providence, now extant, date from 1643. The earlier ones perished in the burning of the town in 1676.* These records are contained in two ancient books, called "the booke with brass clasps," and the "long booke with parchment covers." Only a few specimens can be quoted but these show the mode of proceeding in those days.† Thus: "The 27th 11th mo. 1644. William ffield sold unto William Wickenden all the share of land called six acres lying upon the hill called Fox's Hill, bounding on the east & southeast with the land of Francis Wickes, and on the north & northeast with the highway.‡ On the west and northwest, with Mile end cove on the south with the sea."

This entry is without seal, signature or covenants. It is a mere certificate by the town clerk, to which the whole town meeting were the witnesses. The early transfers,—not deeds, —were mere certificates like this. The boundaries of estates were perishable and liable to speedy disappearance. During many years "wolf traps," or pits and mere stakes or heaps of stones were frequently named as monuments. Black and white oak trees were comparatively permanent.§

" The 14th of the 2d month, 1643, at our Monthly Court, before us the Deputies, we record‖ that William ffield sold unto Thomas Olney, one (ten) acres of ground lying upon the south side of the river called Wonasquatucket, bounding upon the land of Thomas Olney on the east, a mere bank on the south, of the land of Jane Leare on the west, & a slip of meadow of Thomas Olney on the North."

"The 28th of April, 1654. John ffenner sold unto Robert Colwell, the house & houselot which was formerly Richard Pray's, lying between Edward Inman's & John Smith's."

---

*See the report of the town's committee, appointed soon after Philip's War, to ascertain what public documents remained.

†Early Records of Providence, Vol. II., p. 5.

‡Early in this century this was named Wickenden Street.

§Twenty years later the Proprietors became anxious about the evidence of their titles and desired better securities. On the 4th of June, 1666, the town meeting voted that all who desired them, whether Proprietors or twenty-five acre men, might have deeds from the town clerk.
Early Records of Providence, Vol. III., p. 84.

‖Early Records of Providence, Vol. II., p. 6.

Same day, William Burrough acknowledges to have sold unto Arthur ffenner and to Henry.Brown, "one share of meadow lying at Neuticonkonet, adjoining unto Pachaset River, with five & twenty acres of upland lying on the east & on the west side of the meadow." . . "27th January, 1648. Thomas Angell of Providence, sold unto James Matteson, a five-acre lot lying on the east side of the land which Thomas Clement liveth upon, bounded on the east with the land of Benedict Arnold, on the north with the sea, as is manifested by a deed under his hand." . . . This was rare and exceptional. The primitive practice was now changing, as appears by the mention of a deed. These were private transfers. The Proprietor's method was not much more precise. . . . . On the same day, . . "Thomas Harris in the face of the court acknowledgeth that he hath sold unto Thomas Clement that land which the said Thomas Clement now dwelleth upon." No boundaries are given. These open and public transfers doubtless served in early times as a security against fraud and as a preventive of litigation. They also effectually prevented any sales to strangers. "July 24th, 1658, . . Richard Pray hath taken up the sharpe piece of land lying near the place where Richard Waterman's great canoe was made, for a share of meadow, it being laid out by the Town Deputy, it being bounded on the south with a white oak at each corner, also on the north with a white oak at each corner, on the west with a black oak tree." [This was in the neighborhood of the present Steeple Street.] These primitive land owners felt greater confidence in the perpetuity of neighborhoods and homesteads and in the clearness of their own recollections than is common among their descendants in these latter days. After nearly a quarter of a century of experience, they had become aware of the importance of form and accuracy, and the transfers are better specimens of the draughtsman's skill. Whatever was faulty in the work of the conveyancer, was but little aided by that of the "Proprietors' Surveyors." The rude instruments of those days produced boundaries which later generations often found it difficult to identify as those described in their ancestors' deeds. Gen-

erations passed away before these irritating controversies
were laid to rest. To avoid dissentions the Proprietors were
liberal in their allotments to themselves and to their grantees.
By an order of the Town Meeting, then wholly controlled by
the first purchasers,* and which order continued in force
during many years, the rod was to be measured by the
"eighteen-foot pole," both in estates and in highways. This
is still apparent when ancient surveys are re-measured. The
Proprietary grants were small and the "home lot " was often
widely separated from the stated "common lot," or from the
field of ",one hundred acres." Hence, there were frequent
applications from the grantees to the Town Meeting, that is,
to the grantors themselves, for leave to surrender or exchange their fields for others in nearer neighborhoods to
their "home lots." Thus, Roger Williams, 2d June, 1657,
Early Records, pp. 105, 106, asked and received permission
to surrender and exchange his allotment. After thirty years
there was not much improvement. "January 6, 1670-71, laid
out to Thomas Clemence, by John Whipple Sen' Surveyor,
five acres of lowlands more or less, being measured by the
18-foot pole, it lying & being on the North side of Wanasquatucket River, against the place called the Goatom, it
bounding on the south side with the aforesaid Wanasquatucket river, & on the north with the Common, & on the
south east, partly with the Common, & partly with the aforesaid river. It being bounded on the Western corner, with a
maple tree, standing by the aforesaid river side, bounding on
the northern corner with a rock, [which side of it ?] & so as
to range to a red oak tree which standeth by the Wonasquatucket riverside, which tree is on the North side of the river
aforesaid, against the North eastern end of the hill commonly
called Solitary hill. This land in form and manner as before expressed, was laid out to Thomas Clemence for a five
acre lot, due to him from the Towne of his purchase right."
"Recorded by & with the Town's consent January 27 1670-
or 71."† This example shows many of the uncertainties to
which conveyances were then liable.

*Early Records of Providence, Vol. III., pp. 197, 198.
†Early Records of Providence, Vol. III., pp. 161, 162.

Whatever defects or uncertainties of bounds could not be ascribed to the surveyors, were amply accounted for by previous purchases in the neighborhood. The Purchasers' grantees often believed — not without reason — that their lines were overlapped by new grants or surveys. (Early Records, Vol. II., p. 111.) Sometimes reckless or revengeful persons felled the oak trees which were the sole witnesses of titles. The ill-feeling against the Proprietors, which their exclusive claims had engendered, gave too much reason to believe that this was often prompted by malice.* Hence, arose the necessity for penal enactments against any one who had entitled himself to the ancient curse against him who "removed his neighbour's landmark." The willful felling of an ancient tree marked by the surveyor, was an offence often equivalent to the destruction of a deed or the forgery of a record.†

After a few years, the Proprietors and their successors began to complain that their home lots fell short of the legal measure, not reaching the dimensions of the six acres to which each one was entitled. It is observable that the complaint is always of a deficiency and never of an excess. If any thing of this sort were observed it speedily passed from recollection. It was never made a subject of complaint against the surveyors. No offer to restore it appears anywhere upon the records.

These proceedings affected men's titles to their homesteads and were never free from clamor and dispute. As farms became numerous, controversies about bounds multiplied in the same proportion, and a special town meeting might be called for any one of them. At length these became so frequent and wasted so many valuable hours in debates of interest only to private litigants, that the townsmen would not leave their homes in planting time or harvest, at the summons of the Town Sergeant.‡ As a measure of relief,

*Harris says that the small freeholders had borne none of the expenses, burdens and troubles of the first purchasers, and wished to have the same benefits as if they had.

†See Early Records of Providence, Vol. III., pp. 197, 198.

‡So much time was spent in adjusting the boundaries of new grants, and the Town Meetings became such an annoyance, that it was " ordered"

it became necessary to enact that so many as should appear, even at a Quarter-day Meeting, should be a legal quorum. The discussion of these tedious surveys must often have been accomplished in the presence of the ten or even of the seven drowsy freeholders who could be persuaded to attend, in order to save the meeting from failure. The fact that those who had little else to do and whose opinions were of the least weight and value, were often a large part of the assemblage, did not tend to sweeten the tempers of the contestants. It threw the responsibility of the proceedings chiefly upon the town clerk, who was also the clerk of the Proprietors, and thus tended to a concentration of power, perhaps not wholly needless in such an ill-organized community.

During twenty years (from 1640 to 1660), these dreary debates went on about public and private titles, at the Town Meeting and at the town mill. To whom did the Town's unsold acres belong? Little that was new could be said and the old straw was threshed over and over again. Neither party felt more confidence in the Town Meeting Courts, in their knowledge or their independence, than in the "arbitrators" of the old voluntary *régime*. Questions purely judicial, like Verin's, became affairs of town politics. At no period of the dispute did any party propose an appeal to England. They were never anxious to attract the attention either of Charles I. or the military aristocracy of Cromwell, styled "the State." The laws of real property had not been changed under the Commonwealth or under Cromwell, and during his rule some of the ablest of the old Common lawyers, Sir Matthew Hale among them, sat upon the "Upper Bench." Not to mention the costs, the results seemed too uncertain, so great had been the legal irregularities on both sides. The townsmen therefore kept the whole controversy and its issues in their own hands, and contented themselves with gaining such advantages as they might in the Town

27th October, 1656, "that if on the Quarter Days Company appear not according to a former law, then such as meet may proceed to act." October 1, 1657, "because of the often and present great difficulties in getting ten to make a town meeting, that if upon lawful warning, Seven only meet, their meeting shall be legal."—Early Records, Vol. II., pp. 98, 108.

Meeting. There some maintained, as Williams had always done, that his purchase was a "town stock" or public fund, of which the Proprietors were only trustees, although they had usurped the absolute ownership of the whole domain.* This party was numerous among the small freeholders and sometimes had the majority on "the great Town's Quarter day" and election day. They do not appear to have been much restrained in language or to have possessed legal or executive ability. The Proprietors were wary and sagacious and were better advised and led.† Williams and Gregory Dexter, the champions of the small landholders, found an overmatch at all points in William Harris and Thomas Olney.

If Williams asserted that he had intended to create a "town stock" or trust fund, Harris had law enough to answer him, that he had expressed no such purpose in the "Initial Deed," and that a new condition or covenant or construction could not be inserted in it by a subsequent declaration of one party. If Williams claimed that *his* wishes were to be decisive, as to the management of the estate, many were ready with the reply, that *he* had invited *them* into the wilderness and ought to have declared *then* what his purposes were, and not to have kept them secret until it was too late to retreat. They had endured their sufferings and losses, had thrown away all chances and opportunities in Massachusetts and expected to be repaid.‡ They in effect did tell him that he had created no trust and no means of enforcing the application of the purchase money arising from the sale of lots to the uses of the Town. Here was the weak point in Williams's machinery. He could not prevent the diversion of the fund to any other purpose. Courts and Town Meetings, parties and witnesses were all the same persons. They had entered into no covenants and they meant to insist upon the title as

---

*See Williams's "Answer," as he calls it, in the case of William Harris against the Town of Providence. (Rider's Historical Tract No. 14, p. 56.)

†Harris had some law books which he had carefully studied. One of them was "Coke upon Littleton," the great bible of the real property lawers of old time.

‡Harris says (MS. letter) that their expenses in buying off Indian claims were £160 above what they paid to Williams.

they had received it.* There was something to be said, and
it was said harshly and sharply on both sides. Williams had
doubtless intended — we have his constant assertion of it —
that the beneficial enjoyment of his purchase should be coextensive with the town or "fellowship of vote." He looked
forward to a common interest of all the householders in the
ownership of the town lands. Their revenues from sales to
new comers were to be a fund for public improvements, as
roads, bridges, &c., in aid of taxes which must fall heavily
upon a new and poor community. They were not to be merely
the dividends of a private company. But Williams had committed his purchase to a society which could tolerate nothing
but a voluntary association, which could give him no legal
redress. He positively denied that the first purchasers had
paid for any thing but their own homesteads, and maintained
that he had no intention of converting the "town stock" into
a private estate for a mere fraction of its people. His design was far-seeing and statesmanlike, but it passed his legal
skill to give effect to it. It is equally true that he had not
expressed his design in the "Initial Deed" with sufficient
clearness, if he had expressed it at all, and that he had trusted
too far to his influence over his associates. (It is uncertain
whether they knew what his exact purposes were when they
came here. See his letter to Winthrop, before quoted.) They
could reply that his work could not be done without them;
that they had suffered the same hardships; that they were
but ill-compensated for them by small allotments of land
which *he* had valued at only thirty shillings each; that his deed
to them of the Indian purchase should have been made upon
mutual consultation and agreement, while he had only tendered them a conveyance which suited his own theories.†

Williams had probably anticipated the possession of a

*Williams had forced the "Initial Deed" upon them and they meant
to hold him to the letter of his bargain.

†If Williams could quote Scripture as authority in a question of con-
veyancing, so also could Harris. He called attention to the fact that the
words "for the use of cattle," were the same as those used in the book
of Leviticus to describe the possessions of the Levites, which were, according to the law of Moses, absolute and perpetual estates. Leviticus,
chap. 25, v. 34. Numbers, chap. 35, v. 3.

greater authority in the town than had fallen to his share. This was a new experience for him — the attempt to retain political influence in a community which had no religious establishment. Heretofore, he had lived only in States in which religion was supported by law, and he had enjoyed the deference which its officers received from their fellow-citizens. He forgot that only the aid of the civil power had made John Cotton the foremost man in Massachusetts. Some years went by before the effect of his new development was fully perceived, and Williams saw that his opinion was now only that of a private citizen like his neighbors. They had left Massachusetts in order to rid themselves of the authority of the puritan ministers, who, when their reasonings failed to convince, could invoke the aid of the civil magistrates. Williams was not in the habit of consulting with other men or of being influenced by their judgment even when their rights were affected by his action.* He found that to be overruled by a majority, whom he knew to be his inferiors in culture and in experience, was a hard lesson to be learned. It need not surprise us that he sometimes displayed an irritability, natural enough, but to be regretted in a founder and a legislator. He was indignant at the defeat of the cherished project of his life, and he was not in the habit of giving to his emotions any subdued expression. It was not the custom of those days to be choice in epithets when one's feelings were excited, and he was no exception to the fashion of his time. His example furnished a precedent and a temptation to others. Unity, even in matters relating to their own interests, was destroyed.† There were no vessels, not even fishing craft, such as Massachusetts in her earliest days patronized and encouraged. Population did not flow in to avail itself of the freedom of Mooshassuc. Men would not coöperate even in building up the town. As for example : Mr. ffoote, who had learned the craft in England, proposed to set up iron works in a region now known to us as Cranston. Williams favored the project, but the local feuds were so bitter

*See Richard Scott's letter in Fox's " New England's Firebrand Quenched."

†See Bartlett's Colonial Records.

that the townsmen would not join even in this useful work, and the projector departed, it seems, to aid in building up the fortunes of New Jersey. (The Proprietors built no vessels for themselves and would not allow any others to pay a price for the timber or to engage in any commercial business.)*

As might have been expected, there were but few indications of increasing population. Immigrants were not many, and of those who fixed their abode here not many sought admission as "freemen of the colony."†

Even in these latter days the benignity of men's spirits is little increased by so many adverse circumstances. The controversy about the town lands went on, in its only forum, the Town Meeting, and at the only other place of concourse, "the town mill." No practical measure was presented to give a solution to the difficulty. There were only debates which threatened to be as endless as they were useless, and which sometimes proceeded from abuse to violence. Williams was not without skill in the old 17th century art of reviling, in scripture language, and we may well believe that many of his fellow-citizens were not far behind him.

This went on until 1651. The colony was now satisfied that better securities were required to protect it against its neighbors and against itself. In that year Roger Williams and John Clarke were sent to England as agents of the *colony* to obtain, if possible, a new and better charter. Williams soon learned that there was not at that time much hope of obtaining from the Puritan government a charter embodying his own cherished ideas. During many months he persevered in the attempt, and the latter part of his sojourn in England was passed at Belleau, the country-seat of Sir Henry Vane. While there the chief topic of Williams's conversation must have been furnished by the affairs of New England, and he set forth his own views of Rhode Island politics with his accustomed warmth and zeal. At the close of his visit to Bel-

*Weeden (Soc. and Econ. History of N. E.), Vol. 1, pp. 137, 151, cites authorities to prove that vessels were built in Newport so early as 1646. But in Providence there were none until the 17th century was drawing to a close.

†Wm. Harris says, that just before the Indian War (1676), the population of the township was about five hundred souls. (MS. letter.)

leau, which was also the end of his visit to England, Williams persuaded Vane to embody in a letter his views of the conduct and behavior of the people of Rhode Island. The facts on which his censures were grounded were furnished by Williams. Harris and Thomas Olney were not there to modify them or to suggest that there might be another side to the controversy. However partial it might be in setting forth the views of Williams alone, the letter does honor to Sir Henry Vane's feeling in behalf of the distracted colony. It was the sharpest letter ever addressed to the people of Rhode Island.* Vane keenly reproves them for their "divisions," "headiness," "tumults," "disorders," and "injustice," and asks, "Are there no wise men among you? No public, self-denying spirits that at least upon the grounds of public safety, equity and prudence, can find out some way or means of union and reconciliation for you among themselves before you become a prey to common enemies?" He judges that it must be a "high and dangerous distemper" for which kind and simple remedies are ineffectual. He advises the appointment of commissioners to adjust their difficulties. But none such could be found in Rhode Island. Massachusetts and Connecticut were willing to see the dispute go on, in hope to profit by it, however it might end. There were disquiets and disturbances in every part of the colony, and the parties to each were ready to apply Sir Henry Vane's censures to their adversaries. If we should at this day attempt to distribute his reproaches of the townsmen of Providence among those to whom they belong, we might very plausibly ascribe the "headiness and injustice" to the Proprietors, and the "tumults and disorders" to the freeholders of the Town. By being their bearer, Williams adopted and approved the censures. Whether it were politic to expose his own influence to farther attack, we need not enquire. That it had this effect is evident from his own mournful letter to the Town of Providence, written August, 1654. "It is said, I am as good as banished by yourselves and that both sides wished I might never have landed, that the fire of contention might have had no stop in burning." This letter is in Williams's best man-

*Sir Henry Vane's letter was dated at Belleau, 8th February, 1653-54.

ner. He was self-restrained and guarded in his utterances
in public documents. It was in his private acts and writings
that he displayed his ill-judgment. There was one suggestion
in the letter of Sir Henry Vane to which it behooved the
townsmen to give heed. They did so. "They were in danger,"
says he, "of becoming a prey to common enemies." Vane
knew what was going on in England. At the council boards
of Cromwell, Massachusetts and Connecticut were at work to
obtain the revocation of the charter of Rhode Island. If they
were successful, its territory would be divided, and its religious guarantees swept away. All knew that Cromwell was
the fast friend of Massachusetts, and that the danger was not
ideal. The men of Providence yielded to the necessity, and
consented to the submission of one of their controversies
with William Harris to a court named by the Governor of the
United Colonies. They became for a time more restrained
and decorous in their proceedings, and then relapsed into
their old habits.

Sir Henry Vane's letter was addressed to the Colony and
not to the Town, and there was no necessity for the Town to
answer it.* Dexter's reply is evasive. He passes over in silence the disturbances in Providence, and meekly confesses
the sins of Coddington and Dyer in Newport. He asserts
that Providence had always been true to the liberties for the
sake of which it had been founded. This was true enough,
but not relevant, as there had been no complaint against
Providence on that account. Dexter had reason for omitting
the mention of a controversy in which his own share had been
both conspicuous and unwise. Williams's popularity and influence suffered a temporary eclipse, but it revived, for he
was a man too valuable and important to be thrown aside.

As respects the townsmen, much of their turbulence and
their tendency to quarrels and even to outbreaks in the
Quarter-day Meetings, may charitably be ascribed to inexpe-
rience. In Massachusetts, none but members of the Puritan
parishes were voters while the first charter lasted, and the

---

*Williams's letter to Vane was dated August 27, 1654. It was written
by Williams and signed by Dexter as Town Clerk. Dexter probably
made some small additions or changes.

earliest freemen of Mooshassuc numbered among themselves but few of these. The graduates of the English Cambridge and of the American Harvard exacted the deference of the uneducated men, and those who did not yield it had small opportunity of a hearing in the Town Meetings. These were ruled by the fortunate possessors of wealth, culture and sanctity, and a man of humble station had small opportunity to acquire political experience. When some of these withdrew to Mooshassuc it is not surprising that they lacked self-control in matters where their interests or their passions were concerned. Two hundred and fifty years ago experience in public affairs was possessed by comparatively few. The Legislature of Massachusetts was open only to the elect, and the magistrates and elders permitted little adverse debate in parish meetings. There was but one religious society in Providence and that was but a small one. There was no other place for speech or discussion, and in the Town Meeting personal interests and passions sometimes broke over control among these unrestrained disputants. The townsmen were, as a body, more moderate than their leaders, and when they seriously disapproved, their censure fell equally upon Williams and upon Harris, upon Olney and upon ffield, the leaders, both of the Proprietors and of the freeholders. At the present day every school has a society of some sort amongst its boys, and one of their earliest lessons is, the method of conducting the business of a public assembly. Any thing of this kind would have been esteemed presumption by those who practiced the stern family discipline of the 17th century. The future rulers of the Town were left to pick up their political education in the rough school of experience. They did so but slowly in the first generation at Mooshassuc.

The earlier records contain allusions to brawls and disturbances. They sometimes involved the leaders of both parties. One specimen will suffice :* " June 4, 1655," . . " R. Williams, Moderator. Whereas there hath been great debate this day *about* Tho. Olnie, Robert Williams, Jno. ffield, Will Harris and others, concerning the matter of a tumult and disturbance in the winter under a pretence of voluntary train-

*Early Records of Providence, Vol. II., p. 81.

ing, it was at last concluded by vote, that for the colony's
sake, who hath chosen Thomas Olnie an assistant, and for
the public union and peace sakes, it should be passed by and
no more mentioned." It was now June Quarter-day, and this
particular quarrel seems to have kept the town in a ferment
during three or four months. The disputants have left tra-
ces of their ability behind them. Thomas Olney added political to religious reasons for not cherishing a warm affection
for Williams. The irritable temper of Williams sometimes
overcame his judgment, and where pugnacity was required,
whether in word or action, William Harris was equal to the
occasion.

He was not always responsible for such occurrences. The
language used by Gregory Dexter and his party was much more
irritating. But Harris never declined his share in a controversy
when it arose. On this day, Williams had the opportunity of
learning the opinions of his neighbors by hearing a discussion
of his own conduct by such disputants as Harris and Richard
Scott, and of taking the vote upon a resolution which was
equally a censure upon himself, upon his own party and upon
their adversaries. That this particular brawl had begun early
and lasted long may be learned from an entry upon the same
page. [Early Records, Vol. II., p. 81.] "Whereas Henry Fowler
was warned to the court to answer for his marriage without
due publication, and he pleaded that the divisions of the town
were the cause of his so doing, the town voted a remission of
his penalty." June 4, 1655. This was a bold and justly successful answer to the townsmen. From want of religious
congregations, publications of marriages were made in town
meeting during the greater part of the 17th century. This
was the first business in the order of the day. They were
made by the Town Sergeant, whose stentorian voice was
deemed more fit for the purpose than that of the elderly moderator. Henry Fowler was a young man of just twenty-one
years. He had grown up with Mr. ffoote, the ironmaster before mentioned, probably as his apprentice, and still lived at
his house. As he failed to secure a hearing for his publication by the sergeant, he and his friends waited no longer. He
was married without it at Mr. ffoote's house the same even-

ing. His defence in substance was, that the Town Meeting was so disturbed by the fathers of the village that even the publication of marriages became impossible. If they would see the young men respect the law, they should themselves first afford an example. The townsmen accepted the reproof and remitted the penalty. Williams was justly indignant at the conduct of both parties to this affair, at the pusillanimous behavior of the moderator and the sergeant in failing to enforce silence and make the publication, and at the lawless acts of the bridegroom and his friends. This is a specimen of the manner in which men had learned to conduct themselves under the voluntary association in Mooshassuc in the 17th century. This may suffice for an example. Other disturbances arose during the first century of the town. But even when they are mentioned in the letters of Williams, they are charitably omitted from the town record.

Some other discords there were, between Williams and the Proprietors, respecting the administration of their estate. Williams had desired at the beginning that this should be a place of refuge for those "distressed for conscience." The offer, if ever expedient, was so no longer. The Presbyterians asked for no refuge in the colonies eastward of New York. The Puritan had his peculiar abode in New England, where he had become a persecutor in his turn. All sober-minded people who chose to emigrate were welcomed. But Williams did not yield up his fancy that a large reservation should be provided for those of other countries who were in distress of conscience. How a proper discrimination could be made among the applicants, does not appear. Emigrants for conscience's sake, were, in that generation, more extreme and often more turbulent and pugnacious than they are at present. Many could not distinguish between their consciences and their passions. Those who were most likely to come in large numbers, were precisely those whom foreign governments would be least desirous to retain at home. Some had been soldiers, many blended religious notions with those of anarchy and sedition in a fashion now gone by. The "familists" or "family of love,"* enjoyed in their day a reputation

*In the "Dictionary of National Biography" (MacMillan), may be

not unlike that of the emigrants to Utah in recent years. The "fifth Monarchy men," were of very various characters and conditions, for Sir Henry Vane has been reckoned among them. They were not so much an organized sect, as holders of an opinion widely diffused and liable to become dangerous in times when old institutions were breaking up and no one knew what was coming in their place. The conception of government among the men of the fifth monarchy, was a perversion of the biblical vision in the Book of Daniel. After the rise and fall of the four great monarchies, Babylonian, Assyrian, Macedonian and Roman, was to come the kingdom of the Messiah. How was this kingdom to be set up and by whom? It was not clear to all men that the Roman empire was even then at an end, and what means were to be employed to inaugurate its successor? This party had two wings, one ready to employ physical force for bringing in the kingdom, the other seeking to attain their end by peaceful and legitimate means. Of the first description was Harrison, the Parliamentary General, who was willing to resort to the "holy text of pike and gun," for setting up the kingdom of Christ in England. But he stood in too great awe of Oliver Cromwell to make the attempt. Europe had not long before emerged from a religious war of thirty years. It seemed to many that every object, religious or political, could be obtained by military force. There was fighting everywhere and all sorts of fanatics dreamed of accomplishing their purposes by armed insurrection. Their conception of religious liberty was vastly unlike that of Williams. If by any chance they could have gained a foothold here his institutions would have vanished away like shadows. In England a multitude of dazed fanatics, military and others, were ready to join in an uprising which would have ended as such enterprises generally do. They made no general insurrection, but were so strong and restless as to give uneasiness to the Puritan governments, so long as there were any. In such a condition of affairs, it would have been a proceeding of very doubtful wisdom to offer an invitation to a multitude in England who thought themselves "dis-

found an account of Henry Nichlaes or Nicholas, the founder of the "Familists" or "Family of Love," which will give all the information which is necessary.

tressed for conscience," but who had really little toleration for any opinions but their own, and who would have been far more formidable antagonists to the social order of Rhode Island than Gorton. If intelligence had reached London that a large reserve had been set apart in Rhode Island for persons who had suffered from State arrests or prosecutions, and that a sure refuge and maintenance were awaiting them there,—exaggerated as these tales would have been in the transmission,—there would have been danger of a large emigration of anarchists as undesirable as those of our own day. They could come in such numbers that a small and weak colony could neither control nor expel them ; and its institutions if assailed by the fifth-monarchy men, would, in no long time, have been superseded by those of the Massachusetts or Cromwellian pattern. These were the most numerous and most formidable of the fanatical sects of the period. There were others equally ready to gain their ends by force. Men who lived in a steadfast faith in an approaching conflagration of the world, would not have been scared by such trifles as a mere confiscation of property. This danger was not merely imaginary in that generation. The Proprietors would never assent to Williams's proposal of a large reservation for the benefit of "persons distressed for conscience." It was necessary to be assured by their own examination, what consciences they had, and that there were not too many of them. The Town Meeting would never allow Williams or Clarke to publish any such invitation in England. Among Williams's letters of this period is one of unknown date, in which he complains that a tract which he desired to be reserved as a refuge for the persecuted was about to be sold by the Proprietors. Harris and Olney knew something about their own generation in England. They refused to aid a project like this or even to let its existence be known. It is difficult to condemn their judgment. The Proprietors were sustained by the freeholders, and the scheme came to an end.* The Proprietors, however, did make some reservation from their estate, but with views wholly secular, for the relief of the

---

*Thus another of Williams's chief designs in the Plantations at Mooshassuck proved a failure, being defeated by his grantees.

townsmen and especially of the less wealthy citizens. It was designed to afford them some provisions of fire-wood and other domestic supplies, and to allay discontents, to which the Proprietors were not insensible. The only persons to be benefited were the residents of the town, and their bodies only, and not their consciences, were to be regarded. Thus, on the 7th of February, 1658, an order was made in the Town Meeting for certain lands on the Wonasquatucket to be in perpetual common. It was not then carried into effect, "for," says Thomas Olney, "which said order by reason of damage which our Town records sustained in the late Indian War hath miscarried." It appears, however, from some extracts yet remaining from the Proprietors' records, that, in 1658, a large tract of land, containing a thousand acres or more, was "stated perpetually to lie in common." It "embraced a considerable part of what is now North Providence and terminated with the hill north of the Cove and Great Point." This order was lost or miscarried in the Indian wars. But the Proprietors' meeting on the second day of December, 1685, " in view of the necessity of some lands perpetually to be and lie in common, near unto our town for the use and benefit of the inhabitants," . . . "enacted and ordered that all the tract mentioned afore, which was then in common, should forever remain and be in common, and that all parts of said tract which were then taken up, by any person, which should at any time thereafter be laid down to common, should continually so remain, which order was declared irreversible without the full and unanimous consent of the *whole number* of the purchasers." This last was a very common formula, easily disregarded. The reservation was wholly secular in its purposes. It remained entire until the 13th of March, 1724. We shall see what then became of it. (See Town Meeting Records, 1823, Book 9, pp. 279-80. A report of a committee drawn up by the late Judge Staples.)*

*There was now some movement towards the most promising fields in the valley of the Blackstone, but its river was too large for the men of that day. They could not use or control its immense power, and with their humble capital they did not need it, and could not improve it. Their sawmills and gristmills were better served by the narrower streams in the western part of their territory, and towards them was the first movement of emigration.

With all its discouragements the town was slowly increasing, and its population was moving in every direction into the proprietary lands. Chad Brown and others had made purchases of lands beyond the western boundary of Williams's Indian deed ; and had purchased from the native occupants their growing crops and whatever else they claimed. (See Williams's first letter to John Whipple, II. Bartlett's Colonial Records, p. 293.)* Some of these had established their homesteads outside of Williams's purchase and had obtained a title from the Proprietors. As many other colonists had done, they confounded property with jurisdiction and continued to vote in the Providence Town Meetings, although they did not reside within the boundaries of Williams's purchase. They were allowed or encouraged to do so by the Proprietors. In this they were not inconsistent, for they claimed that the whole country west of them was theirs in fee simple, under the second "memorandum" in the Sachem's "deed,"—"up streams "—the streams of Pautuckqut and Pawtuxet "without limits we might have for the use of cattle." The Proprietors were glad of any accession to the number of those who settled in the uninhabited territory, who gave some value to their unsold lands and became supporters of their proprietary title. The Proprietors had always claimed that the words of the "memorandum" vested in them not a mere right of pasturage but a corporeal estate, a fee simple in the soil itself. So long as the population was very small the question excited little interest. The small freeholders who supported the opinions of Williams, had taken it for granted that the soil west of the Indian boundary still belonged to the Narragansetts, and that a new purchase from them would vest the whole property in the *Town* (not in the *Proprietors*), up to the Connecticut line. They were astonished and indignant at the claim of the Proprietors, that it was their own already, and that the inequality of estates and conditions was to know no end. They denied that the settlers on the west side of the Indian line were residents of the Town of Providence, or possessed any right to vote. The constituency of the town was thus drawn in question and a new and yet more heated controversy began. Harris and Olney resolutely con-

*See Williams's letters to Winthrop, p. 330, Narr. Club's ed.

tended that they had acquired the whole territory through
the "Initial Deed" from Williams. A new disputant now
takes a prominent part in the debate.* Gregory Dexter had
received a home lot in 1637, and had signed the first compact
in 1640. He was one of Williams's successors in his religious
society. He was addicted to warmth, if not to violence of
language, and had sufficient indiscretion to ruin any party
which he undertook to lead. In a temporary defeat and un-
popularity of the Proprietors, he had become town clerk,
holding the most important and influential office in the town.
During Williams's absence in England, Dexter, by his fluency
and readiness in public address, became the chief of the party
of the freeholders, and the controversy lost nothing in vigor
and virulence. It had now lasted fifteen years. It seemed
that something should be done for its adjustment, and Dexter felt himself called to do it. As town clerk, Dexter had
possession of the town book, and could insert in it such documents as he thought proper for public information, whether
or not they had been adopted by the town. He seems to have
imagined that he could bring on or force a settlement of this
irritating dispute, and drafted his offensive propositions in
appropriately offensive language. They are not the resolutions of a Town Meeting or in any manner official, but were
for general circulation and for permanence as a political platform or manifesto.

(See Williams's second letter to John Whipple, Rider's
Hist. Tract No. 14.) The "*Sovereign Plaister*" was undoubtedly the composition of Dexter. He alone of his party could
venture on a Latin quotation It expresses the opinion of
Williams and of those who sympathized with him. He de-
clares his approval of its propositions, but is carefully silent
as to the language in which they are expressed.†

"27th 2d mo. 1653. So Gregory Dexter wrote its *Salus
Populi Suprema lex.* An instrument, or Sovereign Plaister, to

*As a printer, in London, Gregory Dexter had been brought into con-
nexion with religious disputants at a time when their strifes were especially virulent. He was not well fitted for the work of a peacemaker in a
distracted colony.

†Early Records of Providence, Vol. II., p. 72.

heal the manifested present sores in this town or Plantation of Providence, which do arise about lands, and to prevent the further spreading of them, both amongst ourselves, and the whole colony, necessary forthwith to be improved and applied, lest this town should fall into grevious sores or gangrenes to the hurt of the whole colony, and thereby, this town, which was the first in this Bay, become the worst, and that only about land in the wilderness.   Per Gregory Dexter (then Recorder)."

After this harsh and irritating introduction of a proposal of peace, Dexter proceeds to give his opinion touching the conduct and claims of the Proprietors.

"Whereas, it doth manifestly appear that all the acts, orders and records which are written in the Town Book are called the Town acts, orders and records, and therefore lawful, binding, &c., of what nature and condition soever they be, whether just or unjust, healthful or hurtful, to the body ; and, '

"Whereas, we upon serious consideration, being the major part of the town aforesaid, finding several acts, orders and records acted in the town's name, to be of this nature and condition, viz. : so destructive to the common benefit and peace of this town, and being so unreasonable, dishonest and unlawful that we cannot according to the rules of common prudence and humanity, but declare against them.   1st. That act to divide to the men of Pawtuxet 20 miles is hereby declared against as unjust and unreasonable, not being healthful but hurtful to the body."*

Upon their construction of the "Initial Deed," the Pawtuxet lands were, in the estimate of the freeholders, as expressed by Dexter, so much taken from the general "town stock" or fund and given exclusively to a small body of Proprietors.   This (No. 1), if it means anything, is a suggestion of a confiscation or resumption of the Pawtuxet purchase.

"2d. Whereas, great and manifold troubles hath befallen both to ourselves and the whole colony by reason of that phrase 'up streams without limit we might have for the use of our cattle ;' for preventing of future contention, we de-

*Dexter forgot that his friend Williams was a party to it.

clare that the bounds are limited in our town evidence, and
by us stated about twenty years since, and known to be the
river and fields of Pawtucket, Sugar loaf hill, Bewitt's brow,
Observation Rock, Absolute Swamp, Orfoord's and Hipsie's
rock ; and the men who were appointed to set it, were Chad
Brown, Hugh Bewitt, Gregory Dexter, Wm. Wickenden, and
furthermore determine that our [construction] (original
writing obscure) of the Deed, and also that privilege for the
use of cattle [from time] to time declared to us, so it shall be
recorded and no otherwise, and no other privilege by virtue
of the said phrase, to be challenged by this town, viz. : that if
the cattle went beyond the bounds prefixed in the said deed
granted to him, the owners of the cattle should be no trespassers, the cattle going so far in one day to feed as they
might come home at night.*

"3d. And whereas, some of us have desired of the colony
leave to purchase for this town some enlargement, which was
granted, and by the great diligence of our neighbour Williams with the natives more land is bought adjoining to the
said bounds, and the purchasers have met and agreed about the
equal dividing of them, as appeareth by their three conclusions ;
first, that all men that have paid equal share shall have equal
in this division of 50 acres to each purchaser, whether they
be twenty-five acre men or other, even so we agree it shall be,
any former agreements or acts to the contrary notwithstanding, and furthermore that all the other acts and agreements
made and concluded upon by the purchasers in their several
meetings touching these lands, betwixt the said old bounds
and *the seven mile line*, is hereby declared by us, so that it
shall be, in all respects, all former or later act or acts, agreement or agreements, thing or things done, Record or Records to the contrary notwithstanding.

"4th. That no disposal of lands, or recording of lands or
changing of lands shall be accounted this Town's acts, unless
the number of 21 of the Purchasers appears and that, only
respecting these lands within the said old bounds *Townwards*,
any former act to the contrary notwithstanding."

*Dexter and his followers did not or would not see that this proposal
(No. 2) would have opened the territory to settlers and purchasers from
Massachusetts, as well as from among themselves.

By this conciliatory proposal it seems that the small free-holders desired to narrow the proprietary purchase to Williams's original bounds, and to make a new purchase beyond it, in which all classes, Proprietors, &c., twenty-five acre men and freeholders should come in on equal terms — rich and poor alike.*

There is a singular inconsistency in the dates mentioned in this document. In Dexter's third proposition, he refers to the "seven mile line." This line was not established until May 14, 1660,† while the "Sovereign Plaister," was presented April 27, 1653. The "Sovereign Plaister" is undoubtedly genuine and of this year, for it is referred to by Williams in his letter to the Town, a few weeks later, in the same year. I can only conjecture that in its original form, it was even more restrictive of the proprietary claim, and that when Dexter and his party learned that it could never be carried through the Town Meeting or the Legislature, it was thought necessary some years later to modify it and to offer a compromise which extended the rights of the Proprietors as far west as the seven mile line, and that the paper copied into the Town Book was altered accordingly. This was not an alteration of a public record, for it had as yet no authority from the Town Meeting. The document as we have it seems to be a revised version of the original. (See Williams's second letter to Whipple.)

During the absence of Williams in England, Dexter had acquired or assumed the leadership of the popular party in Providence. In the heat of political excitement, he had become more extreme in his opinions and more violent in his language. The "Sovereign Plaister" alone remains, by which we can estimate the sobriety of his judgment, and the results of his success. Soon after this paper was put in circulation, Williams arrived in Providence. He was the bearer of Sir Henry Vane's letter, which probably increased the excitement already existing. He could not have been long in Mooshassuc without hearing of the "Sovereign Plaister" and

*This (No. 4) would have made sales and transfers by the Proprietors much more difficult, some times impossible.

†Early Records, Vol. II., p. 129.

its irritating effects. He saw the blundering of Dexter and his party in using language of so harsh a character in a matter which affected the titles and homesteads of so many of the foremost townsmen. [In later years Williams was careful to restrain his approval to the "proposals" of Dexter, saying nothing about their language.] Letter to John Whipple. Rider's Hist. Tract No. 14, p. 37. " What matter of force was there in Mr. Dexter's* *three* proposals for peace and accommodation? Were they not honest, equal and peaceable to any that minded not their own cabins more than the common good of our poor tossed Barke & vessell?" Williams had ample opportunity to observe the temper of his fellow-townsmen as this new documeut circulated among them. (p. 37.) "Our peace was like ye peace of a man which hath a tertian ague. Every other day yea sometimes every meeting we were all on fire, and had a terrible burning fit, ready to come to blows, about our lines, about our lands, and ye twenty-five acre men & purchasers, as yor selves have confessed, &c." Williams saw the injury which Dexter had done to the cause of the freeholders, by his indiscreet zeal in their behalf. In his letter to the Town soon afterwards, he expressed himself as ready to abandon the claims which had been made ; but the author of them did not yield, and Williams to the close of his life was not satisfied of their injustice. (See second letter to Whipple, in Rider's Tract No. 14, p. 37.) The controversy went on as did the brawls in the Town Meeting. If we were to conjecture when the "tumults and heats" of these assemblies reached their height, we may believe that it was upon the very day when the "Sovereign Plaister" was spread between the shoulders of the body politic.†

Notes upon the "Sovereign Plaister." First. The extension of the Pawtuxet lands to the twenty mile line (afterwards the Connecticut border) did not affect any right of Providence men, according to Dexter and Williams's own theory ;

---

*It seems by this, that Dexter's proposals were originally but three, and that the fourth was added at a later day.

†There is nothing in the "Sovereign Plaister," except its rancour, which would not be regarded as unconstitutional in a party platform of the present day.

according to them, the land was open to purchasers. The Pawtuxet men had availed themselves of the opportunity in buying the land belonging to the Indians on the west of Williams's Indian line. This act of the Pawtuxet men saved the land to the colony. Dexter hints at resumption, and Williams says (letter to Whipple), "that some in the Town Street talked about revoking the Pawtuxet purchase, and some said that the 25 acre men had paid an equal peny & therefore should have an equal purchase." Dexter seems to have forgotten, if he had ever known, the legal maxim, "*fieri non debet, factum valet*," or that a public grant once completely vested in possession should ever afterwards be maintained. He did not know that a grant of fifteen years' standing could not be revoked without a shock to all rights of property, which would have been most injurious to the honor and credit of the colony, and perhaps have led to another secession more disastrous to it than that of Coddington. Second. "Up streams without limits," &c. This was an attempt to force the Town Meeting to decide a matter of judicial cognizance only, and to force a re-sale of lands which the Proprietors had already sold. With their lands the settlers west of Williams's Indian line would have lost their rights to vote without a re-purchase. There was something to irritate everybody. The Proprietors were sufficiently indignant already. The "twenty-five acre men," little as they or their boys may have regarded the restrictions upon their rights of common, yet stood by the Proprietors whenever their title was drawn in question. They justly regarded their own expectations of property west of the seven mile line, under the Proprietors' deeds, as worth more than any thing which Dexter could promise them of gains at the Proprietors' expense. They gave no support to Dexter or to Williams. The small freeholders who caused most of the trouble,* had, as Harris says, come in at a later day, and purchased small holdings. They were now clamorous, although they had no

*The Town Meeting could not be persuaded to adopt the " Sovereign Plaister," in its original form. It was not until June 3, 1667, that the Town Meeting " Voted & ordered it to be recorded in the Records of the Town;" with the alterations which subsequent events had made necessary, it was so recorded.

legal claims, having bought their land with all its encumbrances upon it, and having borne none of the burdens of the first planters. The most prominent citizens, as Chad Brown, Wickenden, Abbott, had made no complaints and had not endeavored to repudiate their bargain. The members of Williams's former religious society must have been scandalized by the injurious reflections cast by Dexter upon his fellow-member, Thomas Olney. Some of the Proprietors were also of the society, and a new emotion must have been awakened among them by an agitation equally offensive to their piety and their interests. It may explain what is obscure, through the loss of their early records, that not long afterwards, Gregory Dexter ceased to be an elder, and that Thomas Olney, whom he had publicly charged with dishonesty was chosen in his stead.* Although no practical result came of these contests, yet there was something to excite alarm. There was no check upon confiscation in those days. There had been enough of it in England. There might be here, as appears by Verin's case. The loss of his homestead and investments was threatened, solely by reason of his non-residence. When Olney, Harris and John ffield were forced to unite in order to avert the danger with which Dexter threatened the security of property, it could not be foreseen whose estate might be wrested from him by the Town Meeting.† The Proprietors, however, irritated by the "Sovereign Plaister," retained their self-control and made no reply or protest. They changed none of their methods. There was not much demand for farms or homesteads (See Harris's letter, MS.), but such as there was, the Proprietors were ready to supply it, as if nothing had happened. They went on with their sales and no one hesitated to accept them. Their calm indifference was probably more irritating to Dexter and Williams than any number of resolutions or tracts. However impassive in appearance, they did not forget insults, and nourished their wrath until the time came for its exhibition.

*Benedict's History of American Baptists, Vol. I., p. 478.

†See Early Records of Providence, Vol. II., p. 105. " The Proprietors were in the minority on that day, for Arthur Fenner, the leader of the freeholders, was chosen moderator."

May, 1657. Williams's next encounter with William Harris was one of his own seeking, and was one of the most unfortunate passages of his life. It displayed a vindictiveness, which, notwithstanding his occasional warmth of language, was not usual with him. In May, 1657, while president of the colony, he appeared at the General Court of Commissioners, which was also the highest judicial tribunal, with an *impeachment* against Harris for high treason against Oliver Cromwell. It was subscribed only "Roger Williams, President." He then became the prosecutor as well as the presiding judge. The attorney general (the general attorney as they then called him) did not appear in support of the accusation, nor any one as prosecutor or witness. It was the work of Williams alone, and is an example of his manner of acting without foresight and without consultation or advice. All that is now known of this "impeachment," is contained in a MS. letter from Harris to Captain Dean, of London, of Nov. 14, 1666. Harris says that it contained observations like these : "There had been twenty English gentlemen executed at Tyburn that had not done so much as William Harris had done." He "also shows in his said indictment, what dismembering and disembowelling there should be in such cases." Harris also complains of Williams's perversion and falsifying of his words. He says that "Williams sent a copy of his charges to Sir Henry Vane, who charitably said he thought he was beside himself, and that he did willingly mistake me, saying I was against all governments. It appears that, far before he indicted me for high treason, he indicted me first for contempt of all governments ; and it being demanded whether 'guilty or not guilty,' I answered, 'not guilty.' And the verdict of the jury was 'not guilty.' Yet afterwards he indicted me upon his former ground, for high treason, as being against all government, which falsely he said, in the judgment of the jury. His difference and mine grew by reason of some simple, harmless people that will not defend themselves, but suffer all things ; and will not fight, nor swear, nor take an engagement to any governor or governments, for which cause, Mr. Williams would have sent them to England, for which cause he indicted them ; therefore I wrote to him telling him of his former large professions of liberty of conscience, &c. Whereupon his great wrath and wickedness came forth, and yet remain."

Harris was evidently alarmed. This is apparent from his own letters, and from his last will. In this he used all the skill of the conveyancer to put his ample estate in strict settlement ; avowing his purpose that it should be free from any further danger of forfeiture or confiscation. Harris had good reason for anxiety, for no one could foresee the decision of unlearned judges, swayed by the passions of the people who elected them. It might, however, be safely predicted, that they would take care of themselves, as in fact they did. Impeachment was a popular remedy in that age for chronic political disorders, and Williams thought that it would have a salutary effect in Mooshassuc, by ridding him of his chief political opponent. The court was embarrassed. If reports should reach England, exaggerated as they would be, that Rhode Island was merely a nest of traitors, the story would be turned to account by the neighbor colonies, as a sufficient reason for a revocation of the charter, and a partition of the territory, followed by an establishment of the Massachusetts *régime.* The judges felt that it was necessary to do, or at least to say, something, and speedily adjourned the matter for a full hearing at its session in July, at Warwick. They ordered Harris to appear there, and "doe require the General Attorney to take notice of the case, and to take out a Summons, to require Mr. Roger Williams there to appeare and to make out his charge face to face." Under this grave accusation, Harris was subjected to no restraint, but was only required to give security for his appearance. The general attorney did "take notice of the case," by carefully avoiding it altogether. It seems that Harris had written a "booke" or tract, which was never printed, but which had only been circulated in MS. and which is not known to be now extant. We have no information of the places or the extent of its publication, or of the effect which it produced.

At the July session, at Warwick, Harris appeared. He was a bold man and never hesitated to avow any thing which he had done or written. It was ordered by the court that he should "reade his booke," and Mr. Williams shall "view the original." Probably he accompanied his reading by comments in his sharp and rasping manner. There was no other evidence, and he was called upon for no farther defence. The prudent general attorney "took notice of the case" and was detained by urgent private business, from both sessions of the court at which this affair was pending,—a thing never before or since heard of at the Rhode Island bar. He had too clear a view of the evil to come to the Cromwellian government. What if some turn of fortune should bring the "Kingsmen" once more into power? What would then become of the political fortunes of the office holders in Rhode Island? He kept carefully aloof and the court appointed a substitute. The case was conducted by Williams, although he was president or governor at the time. Williams averred that Harris had maintained "that he who can say, it is my conscience, ought not to yield subjection to any human order among men." This seems to have been Williams's inference from Harris's "booke." As Cromwell's rule seemed then to be the only possible one, whoever denied that denied all human government whatever. Williams imputed to Harris the inferences which he himself drew from the pamphlet. This was the very injustice of which he himself had complained when it was committed by the elders of Massachusetts. The court was ill at ease. The judges saw the expediency of quieting the whole affair and referred the "booke" to two of their own number, with instructions to report upon it by four o'clock the same afternoon. The committee accomplished their task and the court delivered their judgment with tolerable expedition for the heat of a July day. (See Vol. I., Bartlett's R. I. Col. Records, p. 364.) "Concerning W. Harris, his booke and speeches upon it, we find therein delivered as for doctrines having much bowed the Scriptures, to maintain that he who can say, 'it is my conscience,' ought not to yield subjection to any human order amongst men. Whereas the said Harris hath been charged for the sayd booke & wordes, with high treason, and inasmuch as we being so remote from England, cannot be so well acquainted with the laws thereof, in that behalfe provided, as the State now stands, though we cannot but consider his behaviour therein to be both con-

temptuous & seditious, we thought best thereupon to send
over his writings with the charges & his reply, to Mr. John
Clarke, desiring him to commend the matter, in our Commonwealth's behalf, for farther judgment as he shall see the cause
requires, and in the mean time, bind the said Harris in good
bonds, to the good behaviour, until therein, sentence be
given." By this trimming decision, the court decide nothing ;
but the judges are careful to offend neither party, Kingsmen
or Cromwellians. They cast the whole responsibility upon
John Clarke. He was a man of sense, and he "saw cause to
do nothing." Probably these documents never left his hands.
Antiquarian research in English archives has not discovered
them. The loss of William Harris's "booke" has deprived us
of much information respecting the limits of free discussion
considered permissible by the founder of the State. By these
indiscreet proceedings, taken upon his own responsibility
without consultation with others, Williams had endangered
the colony, and he was the chief sufferer. He was not re-
elected as president of the colony the next year, nor ever
again. In later days, when Charles II. had been quietly re-
stored, and the people of Rhode Island were in the enjoyment of a charter more liberal than any which a Puritan
government would ever give, Williams was the subject of
much acrimonious remark, and he does not seem very successful in explaining away his share in this transaction. The
freeholders, whose advocate he was, lost through his indiscretion the support of the Foxians (mostly Kingsmen), during their long control of the government. The prosecution of
Harris, Williams would gladly have forgotten ; but the Quakers, in whom there was as much of the "Old Adam" as in
most other people, were never weary of reminding him of it.*
Inferences very different from those of Williams's were

*The Quakers had good reason to be interested in his case, for
the doctrines imputed to Harris, were not unlike those held by many or
most of themselves. Harris intimates that if it had been in his power
Williams would have banished them from Rhode Island. They were still
but few and weak, but when a few years later, their day of power came,
they remembered the friendship of Harris, and carried him and his party
of Proprietors safely through all their difficulties.

drawn by the Quaker readers of William Harris's "booke."
(See New England's Firebrand Quenched.) These asserted
that he had only maintained that the Parliament without the
king had no claim upon their allegiance. If this were a correct representation, Harris had anticipated by an hundred
years one of the chief doctrines of the American Revolution.
Harris was a "Kingsman," as were most of the Quakers.
They smypathized with Harris, who had the wisdom to cultivate their friendship, and who had their support in future
controversies with Williams.   The warrant against Harris
shows that the chief motive for the prosecution was, his being
a "Kingsman," as were Coddington, Gorton and most others
of that day, who saw in Cromwell only the supporter of Massachusetts and her principles. (See Fox's New England's Firebrand Quenched, p. 282 ; Vol. I. Bartlett's R. I. Col. Records,
p. 361.)

It is impossible to believe that Harris (See Arnold's Hist.
of R. I., Vol. I., pp. 362, 363) cherished designs subversive of
property and magistracy.   His private estate was the largest
in Providence, and he was ever seeking to add to its value.
In his public acts he was always a supporter of law and
organization. The charge of turbulence and anarchy is inconsistent with the whole tenor of his life. The ingeniously
ambiguous statement of the court concerning what might be
deemed treason in England, may be deemed a censure of the
military oligarchy which then bore rule, and which made any
thing treason at its will. Their declaration might be useful to
the judges if the time should come when the times should
change in favor of the Kingsmen. · The General Court of
Trials was not swayed by the passions of the "towne streete."
They needed to be on good terms with Cromwell while his
day lasted, but like many others they saw that it was drawing
to an end and they bade him farewell without regret. [He
died 1658.]

If there were any sense of humor among the spectators of
the proceedings against Harris it must have been a grotesque
exhibition when the chief court of a community which toler-
ated greater latitude of opinion than any other in the world,
engaged in trying one of the chief citizens for high treason
in "bowing the Scriptures."

(Early Records of Providence, Vol. II., p. 112 ; p. 121.) In 1658, the Proprietors had learned that they had nothing to fear from the small landholders. At the town meeting, May 15th, Mr. Olney (one of the chief Proprietors) being moderator, it was "ordered that all those that enjoy lands in the *jurisdiction* [not merely within the bounds] of this town are freemen." This confirmed the right of suffrage to those who had made purchases beyond Williams's Indian line, and indirectly overruled and rejected one of the most important claims in Dexter's "Sovereign Plaister." The Proprietors let the small purchasers understand that they stood in no awe of them. October 27, 1659. "For as much as there hath been a complaint this day, by some of the inhabitants against John Clawson, for making use of the common* (he was a "twenty-five acre man"), it is therefore ordered by this present court that the Deputies or Deputy of the Town, shall forthwith forewarn the said John Clawson to forbear in any wise to make use of *any* of the common." (Early Records of Providence, p. 126.) This was an exercise of discipline without law, over one of the less wealthy freemen. It was both summary and severe. If it were enforced, Clawson and his household would have been deprived of his fuel and fencing material and of many household supplies. At a later day, when the town offered bounties for the heads of wolves and foxes, the small freeholders and their boys, who knew the haunts of wild animals, were thus officially invited into the Proprietors' woodlands. Once admitted they were not easily dislodged and remained there for their own purposes and during their own pleasure. Swine and goats were still turned upon the common to get their living in their own way. As times went on the evil did not decrease and we shall see farther unavailing attempts to abate it.

The harsh invectives against obnoxious Proprietors now so frequent in the Town Meetings and at the Town Mill,

---

*In many English manors there was a custom that a commoner who had put more cattle on the common than his right proportion, might be debarred from commoning for a limited time, and should pay a reasonable fine. But Clawson was a freeholder and a tenant in common, and Providence was not a manor, and had no commoners in the English sense of the word.

stirred up the passions of those who were dissatisfied with
the land titles. These were wont to show their anger by
means wholly unjustifiable.

(Early Records of Providence, Vol. II., p. 111.) Providence,
27th of the 2d month, 1658. "It is *ordered* that if any person or persons shall from this time forward, be so bold and
hardy as to pluck up or break down any bound stake, or cut
down any tree which is the bounds of any man's lands or
between neighbour and neighbour, the said party so offending being complained of to the Town Deputies, or convicted
by two witnesses, shall pay or forfeit to this Towne, the sum
of twenty shillings for every stake, stone, tree or bound, and
the same to be taken away, or distrained of, by the constable
of the said Towne, by a warrant from any two of the three
magistrates' hands, or else whoever doth neglect the same,
either not giving or serving, the Distress of either Deputy,
General Assistant or Constable, shall pay unto the Towne
Treasury, the said money aforesaid."

It seems to have been difficult to enforce this law for the
protection of the Proprietors' estates. Popular sympathy was
rather with their opponents.

During twenty years the Proprietors had urged Williams
to give them a title more satisfactory or intelligible than the
"Initial Deed," and he had steadily refused. He had always
disapproved what he deemed their misuse of his purchase
from the Indians, and would have no farther dealings with
the authors of it. With individuals among them, as Chad
Brown, &c., he had always maintained friendly relations ; but
towards the society and its leaders his hostility was uniform
and constant. They now abandoned hope of any aid from
him, and determined to supply any defects in their title by
ascending to its source. The Indians had now become
familiar with English spirits and gew-gaws, and were ready
to procure them by parting with the lands which they had
held so tenaciously twenty years before. In 1659, the successors of Canonicus gave deeds of confirmation to the Proprietors, such as they had long sought in vain. [These deeds
may be read at large in Vol. I., Bartlett's Col. Records, pp.
35–38, and in Staples's Annals.] It is only needful to say of
them, that they confirm the "Initial Deed" in the sense in

which the Proprietors had always construed it. They convey— to a line twenty miles west of Fox's hill— both lands
and rights of pasture. The grantors were the degenerate
heirs of Canonicus and Miantonomo, and were ready to listen
to any proposals from Rhode Island or Massachusetts, as
their wants or their vices might prompt them. Williams
always spoke contemptuously of these confirmation deeds,
but for a reason which stirred up the wrath of Thomas Olney
and the Town Meeting, and which, if true, would have been
most injurious to the whole colony. It was that the Indians
had subjected themselves to Massachusetts, and had no longer
any tribal lands to convey* (See Williams's letter about
Wayunkeke to the Town of Providence, and Rider's Tract
No. 14, p. 32, letter to John Whipple.)

27th 8th mo., 1660. " The confirmation deeds never received the scrutiny of any royal commissioners or court of
law. Had they undergone it they might have raised troublesome questions about the right of the sachems to dispose of
their tribal lands, without the consent of their people. In
doing this even Canonicus had been cautious and restrained.
As deeds of conveyance, these deeds do not seem to have
added greatly to the security of the proprietary title. They
may have had some effect in preventing farther tampering
with the Rhode Island Indian by the agents of Massachusetts, and by discouraging the attacks of freeholders of Providence who were unable to judge of their validity and who
thus overestimated their value. When they had served these
purpose they were quietly laid away in the Proprietors' archives and were never heard of more.†

*In a MS. letter, Harris says that Williams bought the islands of Pru-
dence, Patience and Hope from Canonicus and Miantonomo, which was
wholly inconsistent with his subsequent claim, that the sachems had no
power to sell lands. Coddington in like manner bought Newport. Massachusetts treated with him, and Miantonomo granted to Benedict Arnold,
lands south of the Pawtuxet River, before William Arnold had induced
Pomham and Soconoco to submit to the English.

†Both the Proprietors and the twenty-five acre men, in their proportion
(one-fourth), were assessed for the money paid to the sachems for their
deeds of confirmation. As they had gained a quarter share in the profits,
so also they assumed a quarter part of the liabilities of the proprietary
shares. (See Early Records of Providence, Vol. II., p. 127.)

It seems that a long credit was needed by many Proprietors, as well as emigrants to the Plantations who purchased
small farms from them. There is recorded in the town-meet-
ing book (27th of April, 1659) a list of "The names of all
such as have paid all their purchase money and have quit-
tances.* During this summer the Proprietors received an
accession to their number, who brought a larger amount of
property than was usual at that day. He, during many years,
aided the Proprietors in their counsels and fought their battles in the town meetings with great vigor and steadiness.
July 27th, 1659.† "This day, John Whipple Senr. is received
into this Town a *purchaser*, to have a *purchase right* of land."
He came from Dorchester, Massachusetts, and brought with
him the Massachusetts notions of property, and of the need
of care in its transmission. He soon became prominent in
the town meetings, and Williams (second letter to Whipple,
Rider's R. I. Hist. Tract No. 14) regarded him as one of the
most troublesome of his enemies. He was licensed to keep an
inn in the days when the holder of the position was one of the
most important public functionaries. His house, on what is
now Constitution Hill, was long the chief political centre of
the town. Town meetings and councils, courts and legisla-
tures often assembled there. He died May 16, 1685.

Williams was now ready to abandon Gregory Dexter's impracticable scheme of confiscation, for he had during some
time meditated a proposal of his own. He had corresponded
with Governor Winthrop, of Connecticut, in order to enlist his
sympathy with the project if not to engage him to take some
share of the lands. The Governor had evidently approved of
the design, and some even hoped that he might be persuaded
to make his abode in Rhode Island, and to become its chief
magistrate. He was a learned man of large and liberal mind
and could have rendered services to the State to which none
of its citizens was equal. The "Planting of a new towne,"
was now Williams's remedy for the disorders of the old one.
(Williams's letters, Narr. Club's ed., 27 Oct., 1660.) The
place chosen was Wayunkeke, a tract in the southern part of

*Early Records of Providence, Vol. II., pp. 31, 32.
†Early Records of Providence, Vol. II., pp. 117, 140.

what was afterwards called Smithfield. Its bounds cannot
now be identified. The new township was to be purchased
from the Indians, as if their title was still subsisting, and
was to contain reserves for persons "distressed for conscience." This project would have led to important results
if it had been practicable. It would have gathered into one
permanent organization a corporation of all the enemies of
the Proprietors of Providence; would have given them two
representatives in the General Assembly, and as the towns
were little subject to its control, would have left Wayunkeke
town meeting virtually at liberty to dispose of the Proprietors' lands within its limits, at its own pleasure. These consequences Williams perhaps did not foresee, as he does not
mention them, but they did not escape the foresight of Harris and Olney. Williams thus sets forth the scheme in a
letter to the town, 27th of the 8th month, 1660. (Early Records, Vol. II., p. 134.) [Extract.]—"As to our new plantation, let us consider if Niswoshakit & Wayunkeke & ye land
thereabout may not afford a new and comfortable Plantation.
To this end, I pray you to consider if the inhabitants of
these parts, with most of the Cowesets & Nipmucks, have
long since forsaken ye Narragansett Sachems, & subjected
themselves to Massachusetts." Williams could scarcely hope
that the Proprietors would consent to a new purchase of the
land which they had so long regarded as their own. But he
had now another enemy on whom he had not counted in former quarrels. Newport during two centuries felt little interest in the town of Providence, or if she ever professed any,
it was only to oppose whatever the plantation at Mooshassuc
most desired. Not until the third of the last century had
passed away would Newport, or any of the southern towns
under her control, suffer a division of the town of Providence
which would add to the political influence of the northern
part of the State Only the colonial assembly could establish
a new town, and any application in that quarter was hopeless.
Besides this, the Quakers were now the rising influence in the
colony, and were soon to govern it according to their own
pleasure, during many years. No party championed by Williams could hope for anything from them.

The Proprietors saw the danger of the theory that the Indians were still the owners of the soil. If they were at liberty to sell it to a new colony from Providence, they could also sell to a new company from Massachusetts, which could easily outbid Mooshassuc, and obtain a foothold here from which they could not be dispossessed, and from which they could be a perpetual menace to Providence.* The Proprietors and their leaders were ever alert and vigorous and they lost no time. Their views and apprehensions are best stated in their own words. This is from the prompt reply of Thomas Olney. "October 27 & 29, 1660, ordered & approved by the Town Meeting, Quarter Court October 27th, 1660. Ordered that upon a writing sent to this Towne by Mr. Roger Williams, bearing date the 27th of October, 1660, that Thomas Olney Senʳ· William Harris & Arthur Fenner† shall draw up a writing in answer unto the said Roger Williams, his writing, and it shall be sent unto him from the Town, and shall be subscribed by the Town Clerk.   .   .   . The copy thereof followeth :

"Sir We received your letter & it being read in the ears of our Towne they considered this answer. That from these words in our evidence taken by you, which are these : The lands upon Mooshausuck & Wonasquatuckett which land, comprehend Musuassacutt Country, are ours already.

"& when we plant there, we will agree with the Indians either to remove or fence. 2 ly Whereas you say the Indians have subjected to the Bay, we say they were subject to the Nanhegansett Sachems when you bought the Land which we now have, and yourself propose yet to buy. And we know that if we let go our true hold already attained, we shall (if

*At this very time the Atherton Company, a Massachusetts corporation, was dealing with the Indians in Narragansett for their lands, and setting up a pretended mortgage upon their territory from the Narragansett Sachems. (1659-60 Vol. I. Bartlett's Records, pp. 429-30; 438-39; 1664, p. 128.)

†Arthur Fenner, who was of the committee to draw up this letter, was one of the popular party and usually acted with Roger Williams against William Harris. He was fully aware of the danger of recognizing the Indian title as still subsisting. (Early Records of Providence, Vol. II., p. 134.)

not ourselves yet our posterity) smart for it, & we conceive
herein that we do truly understand what yourself doth not.
And if your apprehension take place, as we hope it never
will, in those your proposals, we haply may see what we
conceive, you desire not, the ruin of what you have given
name to, (viz.) poor Providence. As for the Natives complain-
ing, we have not yet wronged them, any farther than satisfaction, that we know of, nor shall not, what their wrongs to
us are, we have hitherto rather smothered than complained.
Yet we must tell you that we shall not be adverse to any fair
gratuity, either to take them off their fields or otherwise,
always having respect to the act of the Sachem, whom you
have formerly so much honored. And herein if you can accomplish we shall be ready to assist with further pay, upon
our former groundes, otherwise we shall not meddle, and
forbid any, so to do. Thus in love though in briefe, returned,
We rest your neighbours, The Town of Providence.

Per Me, Tho. Olney Sr. Clarke, in behalf of the Town October the 27th.   To Mr. Roger Williams—These."

Williams was always occupied with the interests of the
Indians and regarded the land titles from their point of view.
He never, it seems, became aware of the danger incurred by
leaving the property in their hands.   He proposed to buy a
second time the Indian tribal lands and offered nothing to
the Proprietors, whose rights he did not recognize. He could
scarcely hope that they would agree for the benefit of other
and later immigrants, who had always been hostile to them,
to a new purchase of the lands which they had so long regarded as their own.   The Proprietors, with the support of
the "Quarter-rights men," had now the control of the town
meeting.   They insisted upon their former claim of absolute
title to the upper waters of their rivers, and would offer
nothing more than a *gratuity* to the Indians to induce them
to remove quietly.   The Proprietors were fully, and perhaps
rightly, persuaded that the maintenance of their own title
was essential to the safety or even the existence of the town.
Besides this it was not certain that the new plantation would
be more peaceful than the old.   So many unquiet spirits, if
they found no subject of dispute with Providence, would read-

ily discover causes of quarrel among themselves. The project of a new town found little favor, and this last attempt at
compromise failed like its predecessors.

The townsmen were becoming somewhat straightened in
their resources, and in February, 1658 (see Early Records,
Vol. III., pp. 21, 22), common was established on all lands
remaining unsold, on the west side of Mooshassuc River.
This was but a partial relief, and available to but few. Something was attempted in the town meeting in aid of a new
plantation at Wayunkeke, March 14, 1661–62. (Early Records of Providence, Vol. III., pp. 19, 38.) "A committee was
appointed to view the lands about Wayunkeke, and to see
where it will be convenient to place a towne & how the towne
shall be placed and in what manner, & to bring in their report." Each of the committee was to have three shillings a
day for his pains. But a farther examination did not confirm
Williams's favorable opinion of Wayunkeke and the plantation of Smithfield was delayed until the early years of the
last century.

It was evidently time for the Proprietors to do something
for the enlargement of the town. Thus far they had only
stood upon the defensive. There were no signs of prosperity.
The western boundary of town and colony were still indefi-
nite. There were no vessels, no fisheries, no market for
timber. There was little profit in anything. Even with the
aid of penal laws, such an estate in the wilderness could not
be maintained. The oversight and police necessary to protect the land against depredation were heavy charges upon
the incomes of those days. The Proprietors could not restrain their own townspeople, much less could they impose
any check upon their neighbors of Massachusetts, who
crossed the Blackstone River and felled and carried off their
choicest cedars. Little redress could be obtained from any
courts of "the Bay." One quotation may suffice as to plunderers nearer home. March 28, 1664. "Continual complaint
cometh to this towne, about the great abuse that is done to
meadows of men in general, which is certainly known to be
done by swine rooting the said meadows up," &c. (Vol. III.
Early Records of Providence, pp. 51, 52, 57, 58.) Then follows

another prohibition of swine on the common land, which
proved as futile as any of its predecessors. By this law of
the town of March 28, 1664, swine were to be forfeited if
found going at large upon the common. The law was repealed
October 27, 1664, " because," as the town records say, "many
inconveniences are likely to ensue." Probably giving occasion to breaches of the public peace. When they could endure
these annoyances no longer, the Proprietors began to look
about them for some better method of managing an estate
which was too unwieldly for the force at their command.
They found it in a new policy, which in later years had an
important influence upon the history of the town and colony.

Down to this time the uncertainty of Williams's Indian
boundary had given inconvenience to private purchasers near
Neuticonkonitt Hill and elsewhere. These things must be
set in order before any new arrangement of the Proprietors'
estate. One of the earliest troubles was with their own
voters. Even the lists of the freemen were not kept with
accuracy. "Town Meeting, March 26, in the year 1660."
(Early Records of Providence, Vol. II., p. 125.) "Thomas
Olney, sen[r.] Moderator . . . Ordered that the clerk
shall draw up the names of the Purchasers and the names of
the five & twenty acre men, and to sever their names distinctly." A landed oligarchy was already formed. It was of
the highest importance that no person should find a place in
the official list of Proprietors who had not a Proprietors'
right or share. None other was entitled to be inscribed
there, and the ordinary freeholder was not permitted to vote
in town meeting upon any question which respected the Proprietors' estate. So long as this distinction was observed,
the Proprietors were secure. The severance between the
names was of importance, both political and social. On May
14, 1660, Town Meeting (Early Records of Providence,
Vol. II., p. 129), "It is ordered by the present Assembly,
that the bounds of this Town of Providence for the first division, be set from the hill called ffoxes' hill, seven miles upon
a West line, & at the end of the West line to go upon a
straight line, North unto Pawtucket River, and upon a straight
line South, unto Pawtuxet River & all the lands beyond

those bounds prefixed according to our deeds,* to be disposed of as this town shall see cause, any former law, or clause therein to the contrary notwithstanding." This was the old "seven-mile line." It was established in anticipation that a new town would some day grow up beyond it, of which it was to be the eastern boundary. It is now the dividing line between Cranston, Johnston and Smithfield on the east, and Glocester, Foster, and Burrillville on the west. With some trifling deviation, due to re-surveys, it remains as it was established more than 230 years ago. The Proprietors had become aware that they could make nothing of their outlying wilderness in the existing state of emigration. They were anxious to disembarrass themselves of these distant woodlands, and to concentrate their attention upon the portion called " Providence Towne," which would be the first to rise in value. No more of the old proprietary shares were to be granted in the new lands, to excite the enmity of twenty-five acre men or smaller landholders. The old Proprietors were to retain all their former authority in the town street. In fact, they gained even more, as no others were to be admitted. The change of policy was not immediate. Every thing moved slowly in those days and especially among an untaught, agricultural people. The townsmen were to be accustomed by degrees to the new system. Those " Village Hampdens" were wont to be somewhat tumultuous in the exhibition of their political feelings, and as they increased in numbers the Proprietors became more anxious to avoid occasions of offence. Not until January 27, 1663, two and one-half years later, was it deemed politic to introduce this resolution : "At a Quarter Court, It is ordered by this present Assembly, that from this day forward, there shall not be any more people accommodated with land as *Purchasers*, within the bounds of this Towne, & that this order be not repealed without the full consent of the whole number of the Purchasers." (Early Records, Vol. III., pp. 48, 49.)

The number of Proprietors had now reached one hundred and one, at which it ever after remained. The society was even now uncomfortably large. Some of its members were

---

*Early Records of Providence, Vol. II., p. 129.

dissentients from the policy of its old leaders, and a new generation could not be expected to be more conciliatory. Olney and Harris must have explained in some manner how the succession of the estate was preserved to those who were entitled to the "fellowship of vote," according to Williams's Initial Deed; but I have found no trace of it. With this "order" there came to an end another design of Williams, that his purchase should be a public trust, to be administered by the future citizens. The Proprietors had long before formed a permanent society, limited in number, and private in its objects. It now was so avowedly. They could act with all needful force and unanimity, as their designs could no longer be thwarted by new shareholders. Some time passed by before they avowed their new policy, and in this instance it was needful to provoke no opposition. But the western line of the colony must first be established before their partition of their estate could begin, and an acrimonious controversy with Connecticut was in the way. Some doubts may have been entertained among the Proprietors themselves as to their new measures, and they proceeded with their wonted deliberation. Their surveys in the wilderness could not be prosecuted in winter, and they had the whole future before them with little other public business to distract their attention. (Very little else of public interest appears on the town books of this time.)

[See Bartlett's Col. Records, Vol. I., p. 417. Providence, May, 1659.] The Colonial Assembly had appointed a committee of four men to mark out the western bounds of the colony and notice was given to Governor Winthrop of Connecticut. Probably nothing had been done as yet under the colonial commission, when the town meeting (Early Records, Vol. II., p. 127. April and May, 1660)* . . ., "Ordered that six men shall be chosen to go next 2d day, come seven nights, & set the bounds of our Plantation twenty miles from ffoxes' hill, westward, up in the country." This was their

---

*Thomas Harris, Sr., was moderator of the April 27th and May 14th town meetings. He was of the party of William Harris and Thomas Olney. The Proprietors evidently had the control of the meeting for their votes of April and May, 1660, effectually destroy the authority of the "Sovereign Plaister," if it ever had any.

only instruction now extant.   The town had no authority, only the colony could act in a matter of this kind.   The townsmen probably erected some monuments to give warning to the colony and to Connecticut of the extent of their claim ; they could do no more.

So closely were their controversies connected with all public interests that every event brought some new dispute between Williams and Harris.   Harris had charged Williams with inconsistency in approving or supporting the establishment of the twenty-mile boundary line, as he had always maintained that the Plantations had no claim to any territory west of the line of the Initial Deed, save a mere right of common "up streams without limits," &c.   Williams's answer was, that he approved the twenty-mile boundary because the Indian Sachems of Warwick had conveyed to the English settlers there lands to an equal distance westward from the Warwick shore.   This seems a very insufficient reason.   It is not easy to discover any rights which could be acquired by Providence by or under deeds of the Warwick Indians relating to another territory.   But the controversy was now closed and could never more be made a subject of debate.   (It was practically decided by the colony in appointing a committee to fix the boundary line twenty miles to the westward of ffoxes' hill.)

After this resolute assertion by the Proprietors, in the name of the town, of their determination to appropriate to their own use the whole of Williams's purchase, he could do no more.   The infirmities of age were beginning to press heavily upon him, and he made little attempt to protract a controversy which threatened to embitter his latter days.   The Proprietors had now been during more than twenty years in possession of the disputed territory, and an attempt to dispossess them might endanger the peace or even the franchises of the colony.   After a delay, which could not have been the pleasantest years of his recollection, he yielded to necessity.   On the 20th of December, 1661, Williams executed a new deed, but not according to the wishes of his grantees.   He now, with the concurrence of his wife, confirms his former deed of 1637, for himself and for his heirs, to the original purchasers by name.* Williams's second deed had a seal and other formalities and a release of dower. But the succession under it was to be in the same society and "fellowship of vote" as before. This point he would never yield, and it does not appear to have been asked of him. The Proprietors already deemed their title strong enough without the second deed, and it was scarcely ever mentioned again. (Williams's first deed. I. Bartlett, 1638, p. 19. His second deed was of 1661, 20th of December. Early Records, Vol. III., p. 7.)

Having approximately fixed the colony's western border and the "seven mile line," which marked the least valuable portion of the territory, and having effectually prevented any increase of their own numbers, the Proprietors went on at their leisure to disembarrass themselves as a society of the western part of their domains. (Early Records, Vol. III., pp. 18, 20.) March 7, 1661. "It is ordered that John Sayles, Arthur ffenner, William Wickenden, John Brown, Valentine Whitman & Thomas Olney Junr shall meet together and order about the division of the lands lying without the bounds which are prefixed for the town; how it shall be divided & in what manner, & what part every man shall have, and to bring in their conclusion unto the town, the next sixth day."† The committee were not neglectful of their work, and on the next "sixth day" it is ordered that, "all the lands which shall be divided, without the seven-mile line shall be divided by papers, according as it shall fall to every man so to stand." A question now arose as to the rights of the "twenty-five acre men." They had much in common with the Proprietors and their votes had carried the Proprietors safely through their controversy with Dexter, Williams and

---

*The whole title of the Proprietors had been in strict law only a possessory one. It was now sufficiently strengthened by the lapse of twenty years, which barred any ejectment suit against them. Williams's second deed was needless. The title was now perfect without it.

†On the same day with an accurate foreboding of the calamities awaiting the town, it was voted, "Deeds which concern this town shall be enrolled in our Towne Booke, and shall also be conveyed unto the General Recorder, to be enrolled in the General Records." A singular confusion of thought, as to the power of town governments to impose duties upon colonial officers.

the freeholders, and they were now to receive the first instalment of their reward.   They had been made a separate class of voters before the "seven-mile line" was established, and it was necessary to make some new provision for them now they had become formidable from their numbers.   The Proprietors fixed the rights of the "Quarter-rights men," apparently without any consultation with them.   They acquiesced as they had always done in the determination of those whom they had always recognized as the true lords of the soil. (Early Records, Vol. III., p. 20.)   "It is ordered that the right of the 25 acre men is, each man a quarter part so much as a purchaser without the seven mile line (paying a quarter part of the charge for the confirmation) ;" [*i. e.*, the money paid for the confirmation deeds of the Indian Sachems] "the which right doth arise by virtue of their commoning, which is within the seven mile bounds, according to the order whereunto they have subscribed their hands.   Only those who were received with a *full* right of commoning *within* the seven mile bounds, are equal with a purchaser without the seven mile bounds, in lands & commoning, paying equal part to the *confirmation*, with the purchaser." In making this dividend no regard was shown to the ordinary small freeholder, who had bought from private landholders.   He had no interest or share in the proprietary estate, and no right to vote in town meeting upon any question concerning it.   The lands east of the seven mile line were henceforth to be more carefully reserved from sale, awaiting the possibilities of the future.   New settlers were welcomed, but to be content with farms beyond the limits of civilized life, unless they were were ready to offer higher prices than had hitherto been given.   At the same time an order was made in the town meeting prohibiting sales of the "common lands" yet unsold in "Providence neck" (Early Records, Vol. III., p. 21) between the Seekonk and the Mooshassuc. This order was not to be repealed without the unanimous consent of the Proprietors or purchasers and no more of the obnoxious "Purchasers" or "Proprietors" shares were to be created.

But much remained to be done, before there could be a division or dividend of lots. A survey of lands in the wilderness went on slowly in those days. There were many rocky uplands which no man would acccept and many brooks and limerocks of which many would gladly become owners. An hundred and one tracts of tolerably equal value were required for the Proprietors alone. Since the beginning of the town, no matter of importance had required the adjustment of so many details. Some were eager for the first choice. It was agreed by the town meeting (February 12, 1665), that William Hawkins and John Steere should have it, provided they paid their dues to the Proprietors, before the drawing.* Roger Williams was to be only the third in drawing. The Proprietors made their own conditions and caused them to be confirmed by the town meeting. "Quarter Day, April 27, 1664." (Early Records, Vol. III., pp. 53, 54.) "It is ordered that 50 acres of upland shall be laid out to every *Purchaser* of this Town, from the 7 mile line *eastward*, and none to be laid out nearer unto this town than three miles from the said line eastwardly, & every 25 acre man to have a quarter part so much as a purchaser, & every man to take his place as it falleth unto him by papers, & none to be laid out until seven months after this day [here follow boundaries]; also what meadow is within this seven mile line, three miles eastwardly as aforesaid, shall be laid out by equal proportions, making distinction between the Purchasers, & the 25 acre men. As also what meadow is found within the seven mile line, that is to say, 3 miles eastwardly from it, as aforesaid, shall be laid out unto every man, answerable unto his proportion, that is to say — the purchasers answerable to theirs, & the 25 acre men answerable to theirs. Also we agree that whosoever pays not in their money which is behind, about the land cleared, shall both lose their money which is behind, about the land cleared, shall both lose his place in choice, and also no lands to be laid out to him, until it be satisfied." Some of the Proprietors were in a low pecuniary condition, and it seemed to their solvent brethren a hardship that these should draw dividends before they had paid the purchase money of their shares. (Early Records of Providence, Vol. III., pp. 66, 67.) The order excited dissatisfaction. It expressed the

*Early Records of Providence, Vol. III., p. 69.

wishes of Harris and Olney and of the most wealthy of the Proprietors. But it created dissension and threatened farther delay. It was repealed in great part in the following January. (Vol. III., Early Records, pp. 66, 68.) Another example of the want of stability of the early legislation of the town. The limerocks were to remain in common. (Early Records, Vol. III., p. 93.) All difficulties being overcome the Proprietors drew another line, three miles nearer to the town of Providence. This line was called the "four mile line," and the territory was called the "second division" or "fifty acres division," situate, lying and being between the "seven mile line" and the "four mile line," set by order of the town of Providence. Nothing since the planting of Providence had furnished so much business to the town meeting, had been so often postponed, or fills so much space in the records. (Vol. III., Early Records of Providence, February 19, 1665, pp. 72-74.)

The great day came at last. There was no lack of a quorum at the inn where the freemen were assembled. The Proprietors or purchasers under Williams's deed, who held the entire unsold fee simple of the town — the "twenty-five acre men," longing for some increase of property and for a corresponding rise in the world, and rightly regarding this as an earnest of other like benefits to come — the small freeholders who had little more than small lots or gardens purchased of some more prosperous owner, who had found small profit in holding them or who had left the town, and who could only look on as spectators of a ceremony in which they had no share, were all, with very different feelings, eager for the great event of the day. Curiosity to see what was coming preserved order. Before the formalities began there arose in the midst of the assembly, the gaunt and picturesque figure of the founder. Age and infirmity were already pressing heavily upon him — the burden of his long and laborious service of the colony. In the presence of them all he "witnessed" — not now against the usurpation of the Proprietors, of which he was partaker, but against the "prophaning of God's worship by casting lots." He had no more to say, at least in public, of "up streams without limits," or of the "fellowship of vote." All these questions he knew had been decided against him, if not judicially, yet by public opinion ; and he urged them upon the town meeting no more. Few others saw any caricature, still less any imitation of divine worship, in this eager grasp after prosperity. We may well believe that all smaller matters, even the publications of marriages, were hurried through without ceremony, and that the great business of the day was speedily begun. The solid men of the plantation, the Proprietors and purchasers, claimed the first attention. Ninety-three of these "drew papers" for lots east of the "seven mile line." Among the earliest of those who "drew papers," was Gregory Dexter, although the whole proceeding was in contravention of the doctrines which he had for so many years maintained, and was wholly subversive of his favorite "Sovereign Plaister." Williams, whose conscience was in a disturbed condition, and one Reddock, who was charged with not paying his dues, were given leave to draw their shares at a future day. The remaining six Proprietors, to whom no such opportunity was given, may have shared in Williams's scruples or may have been in arrears with their payments. Next in order were the "twenty-five acre men." They received their portion at the second table, as it were. But they made no complaint, satisfied that their investment in quarter shares had been so far a good one, and with an added opportunity of helping themselves from the Proprietors' common. The small freeholders offered no opposition, looked on with such edification as they might and reserved their wrath for town meeting and election days. They were well aware of the advantage which the early institutions of the town gave them. None of the deeds of these shares could be recorded, except by vote of the majority in town meeting, and the irate majority resolutely withheld their consent during several years. Their doings at elections we shall presently relate.* At the session of the Assembly at Newport, after the spring election, two delegates presented themselves from the town of Providence. There had been two town meetings and two town clerks. William Harris and Arthur Fenner the "assistants" of Providence had generally been

*See Bartlett's Records, Vol. II., 1667, p. 200.

opposed to each other in town politics and had probably called the rival town meetings. The "assistants" were also *ex-officio* members of the town council. Only the meeting called in the interest of the Proprietors was recognized by the General Assembly or has any record in the town book. William Harris and Arthur ffenner appeared as champions of the opposing parties, and charged each other with "rowtes" at the elections. The proceedings are briefly recorded and were closed by a letter of admonition from the Assembly to the town of Providence. The whole affair reached only this "lame and impotent conclusion."

The letter of the Assembly had little effect in calming the heated passions of the townsmen. The details are not preserved but we can readily comprehend what followed in the "Towne Streete," by the proceedings of the General Assembly. Williams next tried his skill in peacemaking. (Town meeting, March 8, 1668.) "Voted that the presentation in verse, presented by Roger Williams unto the Towne, this day, be kept among the Records of this Towne." The verses had but a brief existence and perished in the burning of the town. This was not the least valuable document lost in the Indian war. Why may not this precedent be revived, and this unworked vein of poetry be re-opened? If there be among us youthful aspirants for immortality, why should they not address their strains to the Common Council? Perhaps even the Board of Aldermen may be so softened as to yield unlooked-for answers to their requests.

Some extraordinary remedy seemed to be demanded by the disquiets of Providence. At the General Assembly in May, 1669, it was "Ordered that Mr. John Clarke be requested to write unto the inhabitants of the Towne of Providence, to persuade them to a peaceable composure of that uncomfortable difference that is between them." Mr. Clarke could have told them, that those who had granted the charter of the colony had already seen their mistake and would welcome any opportunity to take it away. (Bartlett's R. I. Records, Vol. II., pp. 288, 289, 293, A. D. 1669.) This well-meant endeavor failing like its predecessors, it became difficult to forecast the future.

The contentions about the proprietary lands were all the
while going on. (Early Records, Vol. III., p. 136.) February
15, 1668. Arthur ffenner Moderator. "The bill presented by
Henry Browne, Thomas Hopkins Senr & Shadrack Manton is
excepted, that each person may take up their land according
to the former order, without prohibition of common. Voted
& ordered that the former bill is excepted (*i. e.*, refused) in
giving liberty that all common shall be free without any
prohibition."

There is little that is pleasant in these details of town
affairs. The strife went on until 1669, the disorders of the
town meeting apparently increasing, until the freeholders
seemed ready for another violent outbreak like that in Gorton's time. Their cause was just then severely injured by
their old champion Gregory Dexter. His conscience had now
become so tender that he refused to pay taxes for the support
of government. William Harris had not forgotten Dexter's
"Sovereign Plaister," of sixteen years before, which had stig-
matized himself and his brethren with dishonesty and oppres-
sion. He eagerly seized the opportunity to retaliate upon his
old opponent and to prove that he and the Proprietors were
the only upholders of property and law. In Harris's conduct
there was always more of the *fortiter in re* than of the *suaviter
in modo*. Procuring a lawful appointment he levied the tax
upon Dexter's estate. The vigor and severity of his proceedings gave occasion to Williams to speak with equal censure
of them both.* The partizans of each doubtless concurred in
Williams's disapproval of their adversary. The letters to
Whipple were apparently of a semi-public nature, being intended to be read at Whipple's Inn, the great centre of information in those days.

The confusion in Providence had now reached such a
height that the legislature became alarmed. They saw that
the discords of a single town were endangering the privileges
of the colony. The evil days described in Sir Henry Vane's
letter seemed to have returned. Such disorders unchecked
would cause the forfeiture of the charter, and nothing like it
could be hoped for again. The Assembly at Newport (27th

*In his letter to John Whipple.

October, 1669) determined at last to make some show of firm-
ness. On the last election day, two town meetings had been
assembled in Providence, each with an official calling himself
the town clerk. As usual, only the meeting which represented the Proprietors has any record in the town book. The
clerk of one meeting certified that there had been no election;
of the other, that deputies had been duly chosen. It seems
that the day was not ended until there had been a resort by
angry partisans to arguments more forcible, if not more con-
vincing, than those of mere words. The legislature refused
to receive the deputies from Providence as not being duly
elected, and then made an earnest endeavor to secure peace.
Probably, the Quakers of Newport prompted these efforts.
"The General Assembly sadly resenting the conduct of its
oldest town, & expressing its alarm at the grievous symptoms
that appeared, of the dangerous contests, distractions, & divisions among our antient loving & honored neighbours, the
freemen & inhabitants of the Towne of Providence, whereby
the said Towne is rendered in an incapacitie for transacting
their own affairs in any measure of satisfactory order, with
peace & quietness, & consequently unable to help in the
managing & ordering public affairs by Deputyes, that ought
to be by them sent to the General Assembly, and jurymen
to the Court of Tryalles, whereby there is, or seems to be a
breach in the whole ; upon consideration whereof, & upon
finding that the case of the said inconveniances ariseth from
disagreement & dissatisfactions about divisions & dispositions
of landes, wherein it is impossible that either party can be
clear from giving & taking occasion of offences, and it is
altogether unlickly they will compose the differences, without
some judicious men and unconcerned in the premised contest be helpful by their counsell to that end." The Assembly
thereupon appointed five commissioners and requested and
commissioned them to proceed to Providence, and there to
endeavor to persuade the parties to an arbitration, or to call
a meeting of the freemen, and to hold a meeting of *all* the
freemen, and to elect town officers and town deputies to the
Assembly (p. 287, &c.). "And to the end that it may appear
how much we desire the same, the Court doe order that all

indictments or actions which have arisen, concerning or having relation to the difference aforesaid in the Town of Providence, shall be waived at present & no farther prosecution be
therein, until the Assembly shall meet ;" . . "hoping in the
mean time that all animosities will be extinguished."*

This well-intended scheme utterly failed. At the March
session in Newport (1699, pp. 292, 293), the Assembly appointed two commissioners to ascertain who were the legal
voters of Providence, and to hold an election for deputies to
the May session.

The general sergeant of the colony was directed to be
present, but we are not informed as to his ability to enforce
his commands. The labors of the colony's five commissioners were in vain. Neither the Proprietors nor the twenty-
five acre men would make any compromise which would
involve the title to their estate. The irritation of the small
freeholders was equally extreme.

The commissioners appointed from the leading citizens of
Newport, visited Providence and strove, with such eloquence
as was at their command, to accomplish the benevolent design of the Assembly. The townsmen were not accustomed
to pay much deference to the wishes or the exhortations of
Newport. They were too near to the days of Coddington's
secession and remembered too well the readiness of Newport
to abandon the first principles of Rhode Island and to subject herself to Plymouth. The disorganization of Providence
had proceeded far. The town could hold no election, and now
during several months there had been no town clerk, treasurer, sergeant or constable. The townsmen were left to their
own discretion and self control, which (as appears from the
numerous indictments then pending) could not always be
trusted. The only town authority then remaining, the town
council, took possession of the records and only delivered
them up to John Whipple, when duly elected. (Early Records
of Providence, Vol. III., p. 151 ; pp. 149, 150; December 15,
1669.) Newport was now under the political control of the
followers of George Fox. We may imagine the effect of a
moral lecture given by a committee of Foxians to the adherents of Roger Williams.

*Vol. II., p. 292, Bartlett's Col. Records.

At the election holden by the State officials, William Harris and Arthur ffenner were candidates for the place of second assistant. There was a difference of opinion among them, as to which had been elected by the majority of qualified voters, and "they both being not very free to accept upon such doubtful tearmes, thereupon by the Assembly, Mr. R. Williams was chosen assistant." In reading the memorials of these by-gone controversies we may see cause to be glad that the Plantations had sent forth no encouragement to the religious enthusiasts of the 17th century, who imagined themselves "distressed for conscience." Not many of them favored the settlement of controversies upon principles of peace and non-resistance. It would be difficult to estimate the consequences if the crowds who thronged the meetings of Fox and Burnyeat had been favored with discourses from the expectants of the " 5th monarchy," or of the "family of love."

Though the adjustment of the quarrel in 1669 decided in express terms no principle of colonial law, yet it was effectual and final. It was felt by both parties that the success of the Proprietors was complete. The Assembly would do nothing in aid of the small freeholders who were the partisans of Williams. No interest which claimed as its champion the author of "George Fox digged out of his Burrows" could hope for any thing from the Foxian legislature at Newport, and the Proprietors were now well assured that they could appropriate Williams's Indian purchase at their pleasure. They went on accordingly, first to remove any clouds upon their title. During sixteen years, the "Sovereign Plaister" had remained upon the town records, as it had been inserted there by Dexter, without any authority but his own. The Proprietors had taken no notice of its injurious assertions. It seems probable that they would have continued to disregard it. But it appears to have been quoted in the General Assembly at Newport as evidence of the public judgment of Providence. On the 15th day of December, 1669 (Early Records, Vol. III., pp. 148, 149), the town meeting was once more assembled. The Proprietors were in the majority, for Thomas Olney, Jr. (their

life-long champion), was moderator.   William Harris, also,
was not "wanting to the meeting." On that day it was "voted
& ordered, that whereas this Assembly having received information that there is a record in our Towne Booke, in the
126 & 127 pages of that Booke, wherein is the Combination,
which record is a writing entitled an instrument or Sovereign
Plaister, and was endorsed Thomas Clemence, the Towne
having viewed a copy of the sd record, & considering the
same, the matter therein, doe find it to be the most destructive to the peace of our Plantation, & the joint agreements
of our Towne, & the orders thereof, the which, the Towne
taking into serious consideration doe find the said matter to
be utterly unwholesome & illegal, and doe hereby declare the
said record to be wholly void, null, any agreement order
or record at any time made, or any clause therein, to the
contrary notwithstanding."   This *was* an authentic record
never revoked or questioned by the town.   It put an end
to attempts by the freeholders to defeat the wishes or
acts of the Proprietors.   Henceforth they administered their
estate in their own way for what they deemed to be their own
advantage.   Gregory Dexter could not have looked back with
much satisfaction over his sixteen years' labor.   He had committed a gross impropriety by inserting in the town book a
private document of a libellous character, without any authority but his own.   The vote of the town meeting was official
and authoritative, and there was no hope of its reversal.   The
"Sovereign Plaister" was never heard of more.   The foresight of William Harris in cultivating the friendship of the
Quakers and of a class of small proprietors,—the twenty-five
acre men,—in union with the larger, had accomplished its
office.

(Early Records of Providence, Vol. III., p. 156, 27th July,
1670.)   The dissatisfied freeholders were not the only com-
plainants.   The unskillfulness of the early surveyors, and the
tardiness of their action, caused loud complaints among the
Proprietors themselves.   Some of them found other shares
overlapping their own or intruding into their place.   No notice seem to have been given of the times of laying out the
meadows, and the usual irregularities ensued.   Not until the

interference of the town meeting did it seem possible to accomplish the work with speediness and peace. The usual quarrels about the boundaries of farms seem to have superseded quarrels over controversies of greater moment.*

Nothing of historical interest occurred during the next two or three years. It seems that those who participated in the dividend of lots, were not all of them satisfied with the result. In 1672 there were rumors that another was in contemplation. It was not viewed with gratification by those who could only look on while the town lands were divided among a limited number of the older inhabitants. Old grievances were not yet allayed. In view of what had passed, Edward Smith, of the family at the Town Mill, addressed his counsel or remonstrance to the town meeting. He had begun life as a "twenty-five acre man," but when he prospered he had acquired a "Proprietor's share." He held liberal views of the policy to be adopted in dealing with the different classes of landholders. (Early Records of Providence, Vol. III., pp. 225, 226.) 27th January, 1672. Mr. Arthur ffenner, Moderator, ... Voted that the bill presented unto the Towne by Edward Smith, shall be put upon the records of the Towne, & that each man's land, according to the desire made manifest in that bill, be recorded in the Towne Booke as their lawful right and inheritance, to them & their heirs, forever. Providence, the 27th of the 11th mo., 1672. This was Edward Smith's "proposal." "A reasonable, seasonable & ready way of encouragement to Planters in their labour in this our Plantations, of Providence, presented to the Town Meeting.

"Neighbours : Whereas there has been, & yet is, an uncomfortable difference in this towne, about a new division of lands, which you all sufficiently know, and in the time of this difference both sides hath laid out 50 acres to divers men, & some of these lands are known to be relaid, & more feared, which proveth a great discouragement to laborious men, for encouragement therefore to the industrious, do you, my neighbours, resolve, determine, these two things : first, that all these several shares of land, laid out in the new division to Planters, by both sides, shall stand, which shares consist-

*See petition of Epenetus Olney and the town order upon it.

ing of 50 acres, less or more, not exceeding 60, & that
Planters on both sides to whom the said 50 acres was first laid
out, that land shall be his proper right, whether the said re-
laying by either side was wilfully, ignorantly or under what
pretence soever done, any former act or acts, thing or things,
record or records made to the contrary notwithstanding.
2d^{ly}, that provision be made for recording the said 50 acre
shares in the Town's booke, to those men to whom they
were *first* laid out, so much of the forest to be suddenly
subdued by the laborious, & become a fruitful field, which is
the desire of your neighbour, Edward Smith." It appears
from this statement of the difficulty, that some of those who
were disappointed in the shares which they had drawn, had
caused them to be " relaid," in more desirable places, taking
to themselves many of the best sites — that some of the Proprietors held tenaciously to their newly acquired lots, neither
selling nor cultivating them, and that immigration of "laborious men " was discouraged. The poorer townsmen found
it no easier to acquire lands than it had been before. As no
land transfers or titles could be perfected in those days without a vote of the town meeting, allowing them to be recorded,
the dissatisfied party among the townsmen had thus found
means to delay during several years the registration of the lots
drawn by obnoxious Proprietors.* The Proprietors who had
"relaid" or exchanged their shares, were by the resolution
of Edward Smith, remanded to their original drawings. No
farther hindrance was to be given to their registration. This
power of a town meeting over freehold estates, thus summa-
rily exercised at the request of Edward Smith, gives a view
of the despotism of a landholder's government in those days.
Arthur ffenner was the chief of the liberal party. His election as moderator shows that they were in the majority at
that meeting. The adoption of Edward Smith's resolution,
proves that all parties were now resolved to avoid further
contention upon this subject and that the Proprietors had

---

*None but the Proprietors were entitled to vote upon matters concern-
ing the proprietary estate, but when lots had been drawn by individuals,
they ceased to be parts of the proprietary estate, and were subject to the
votes of the entire body of small freeholders.

gained in substance all that they had claimed. The kindliness of spirit manifested by Edward Smith, probably gained the adoption of his proposed compromise. The dividend was confirmed, all lots were now to be secure, but only as they were at first drawn. A dissatisfied Proprietor was not to be permitted to exchange or "relay" his drawing, and thus to select for himself one of the most desirable homesteads, instead of the chance benefit of the lottery. Even a Proprietor might be displeased at the greediness of some of his brethren, who, having drawn what they considered little better than blanks among the Proprietors' chances, made that a pretext for helping themselves to the finest sites in the Plantations. Perhaps the unanimity in adopting Edward Smith's resolution may be in part thus explained.

So great a dissension had been created by the first dividend that some years elapsed before there was an attempt at another. The Proprietors waited until 1675. They had established yet another division of their estate, "situate, lying & being between the seven mile line & the four mile line set by order of the Town of Providence." In order to pacify every one, on the 6th of April, 1675, it was "Voted & ordered that unto *every one* that hath a right in those lands beyond the 'seven mile line,'* set by the Town of Providence, shall be to each right one hundred & fifty acres of upland, laid out to them, any law or laws formerly made to the contrary notwithstanding." It does not appear whether the "twenty-five acre men" were becoming unquiet again. The designation had now become inapplicable and little more is heard of them in that character.

On the 12th of April, 1675, eighty-one Proprietors "drew papers" for fifty-acre lots *west* of the seven mile line. The business was not then completed. On the 24th of May, 1675, the Proprietors alone "drew papers" for lots between the "four mile line" and the "seven mile line." There were ninety-five proprietors living eastward of the seven-mile line. They did not then hanker after estates in the near neighborhood of an Indian frontier, even although they were to be had for nothing. It was long before they were offered another oppor-

*This included the twenty-five acre men.

tunity. At the dividend in April, 1675, a protest was offered in behalf of Joshua Verin, by Thomas Harris, Sr., and Thomas Olney, Jr., Epenetus Olney, and John Whipple, asserting his right to a Proprietor's share, which, it would appear, some of the townsmen still wished to subject to forfeiture for non-residence. More enlightened views of property were now prevailing, and Verin was allowed his claim as one of the original planters of Mooshassuc.* Little else occurred during the present year. There was little or no excitement about the "draught." The final adjustment of their rancorous old quarrel was drawing near, in the natural order of events.

The Narragansetts were already restless and little was needed to provoke a general uprising of the New England tribes. The following order may show the state of affairs in Providence. Town Meeting, October 14, 1675. Arthur ffenner, Moderator. "Ordered that six men every day shall be sent out of the Towne to discover what Indians shall come to disquiet the Towne, and that every housekeeper and all men residing in this Towne shall take his turn, & he that shall refuse to take his turn, shall forfeit to the Towne for every day's default, five shillings, and that it shall be taken by distraint, by the constable and that this order shall stand in full force until the Towne order to the contrary." The end was already near when the town meeting imposed this heavy burden. The weak and vain Canonchet, disregarding the counsel of Williams, set about to establish a military reputation for himself. The manner in which he did it belongs to the history of the State.† In due time came the ravaging of Narragansett and Coweset, and, in March, 1676, the burning of Providence. Suffice it to say, that with their habitations there perished most of the property of the planters. For the moment the hopes of the townsmen seemed to be at an end. Some of them left Providence, never to return. It offered few inducements to settlers during many coming years. When it revived, a tax of £:ა was deemed sufficient for its ability, while Newport had

---

*The names of those who "drew papers" for shares of land west of the seven-mile line are given in the records of 24th of May, 1675.

†Dr. Stone has so thoroughly investigated the subject of the burning of Providence that it need not be done again.

lost little or nothing. Those who came back to rebuild the town were chiefly the first planters at Mooshassuc and at Pawtuxet and their families. These were the depositaries of its earliest traditions and they raised it up anew upon its old foundations. In the general ruin there came, almost for the first time, a period of union and peace. Even Williams and Harris could act together in a committee for the disposing of Indian slaves. While some were removing to other and stronger colonies, the Browns, Arnolds, Angells, Olneys, Carpenters, Rhodeses, came back to do their work over again, and they did it effectually. The old Proprietors were still recognized as the legitimate rulers of the town, and long years after the rebuilding, they were still as rigid as their fathers in their scrutiny and rejection of applicants for the "fellowship of vote," and for permission to purchase lots and to become inhabitants. One or two examples will suffice: 1681-2. "Voted & Granted unto William Hudson formerly an apprentice to Joshua ffoote, leave & liberty to buy land of any free inhabitant of this towne, & settle among us." "It is granted unto Daniel Jenckes that he hath liberty of the towne allowed him to dwell & abide with his brother Jenckes whereby he may learn & perfect his trade at his brother Joseph Jenckes."

With the revival of the town, some of its old troubles reappeared in full activity. Organized opposition to the Proprietors now sunk into displays of private malice. As before the war in 1676 there were (11th March, 1675-6) many intruders and trespassers upon the newly opened lands west of the seven-mile line. Four persons were appointed to warn off and to remove trespassers. It was necessary to bring the whole tract into private ownership. ffenner Smith, Ephraim Carpenter and Thomas Olney, Jr., were of the first who filled this undesirable office. How long this frontier police was maintained does not appear.

Some unexpected consequences followed the Indian war. The colony recognized no successors to king or sachem. There was no longer any fear of their bargains or alliances with Massachusetts. No Indian claims to lands were any longer regarded. The fields "up streams without limits" were now the fee simple of the Proprietors, as Harris had always maintained. There was now no Indian chief whose title deed would have been sought or accepted, and all fears of a new purchase from them, west of the plantations, were dispelled. Henceforth the colony knew the Indians only as tramps and vagrants, and at a later day (when they had ceased to be Indians and were becoming negroes) — as wards.

Other influences were coming in of which the former generation of townsmen had known nothing. Charles II. had now been several years upon the throne. Republicanism was crushed and silenced for a century to come. The golden age of the English aristocracy had begun. The English Revolution of 1688-9 carefully kept itself free from every taint of democracy or equality. Property now ruled instead of Puritanism. No voice from English literature or politics gave sympathy or encouragement to the principles upon which American society had been founded. Governments were everywhere harsh, peremptory, based everywhere upon landed estates or military force. The so-called English Commonwealth had been no exception. In such an age the society of Proprietors of Providence was not obsolete or antiquated, or necessarily unpopular. It was not possible to set up any tolerable imitation of English political institutions on this side of the sea, but the colonies found no difficulty in forming an oligarchy in accordance with their own wealth and their own notions. In fact, municipal corporations everywhere were ruled by contrivances very like in principle to those of the purchasers of Providence. There was no democratic party anywhere. The newest religious party was that of the Quakers. They were monarchical in their tendencies and earnest seekers after the good things of this world. They had their own way in Rhode Island.

It will suffice merely to mention the Proprietors' dividends of the following years. On the 17th day of March, 1683-4, draughts were made for shares of land west of the seven mile line, among the proprietors, including Joshua Verin. One hundred Proprietors, Roger Williams, 2d, among them, drew lots. He had, it seems, reconsidered his father's scruples, and took his share with the rest. Perhaps he reasoned that as the Narragansetts were now extinct, he could, with a good conscience, claim his part in their inheritance. Changes were now passing over the plantations at Mooshassuc. The older generation who had borne the burdens of its early years was passing away. Williams came no more to the town meeting and Thomas Olney was no longer heard at the Town Mill. Harris died alone, but, we may trust, not without friends, in a foreign land. With the old party leaders much of their bitterness passed away. The questions over which they had quarreled had found their own solution. The new age had interests of its own. They did not fight over again the battles in which their fathers had worn out their lives. The Indian war had left behind it a plentiful crop of troubles in every town. Their Indian land titles had been far from satisfactory and did not improve in value in the hands of speculators from Massachusetts. The present moment of peace and goodwill seemed an appropriate one for closing all controversies over them. The opportunity was readily seized, and was handled with a skill which would haved done no discredit to modern politicians. The Quakers had control of Newport and its dependencies, of which they were the chief landholders, and they sympathized with the friends of Harris. Each town was to have what its great men wanted. In 1682 an act passed the Assembly at Newport on the 3d day of May, entitled, "An act confirming the grants heretofore made by the inhabitants of the Towns of Newport, Providence, Portsmouth, Warwick and Westerly, and to enable said Towns to make prudential laws and orders for the better regulating their Town affairs."

"Whereas in the 15th year of the Reign of our Royal Sovereign Lord Charles the 2d of Blessed Memory, there was a Charter granted to this his Majesty's Colony of Rhode Island & Providence Plantations in New England, in which was contained many gracious privileges granted unto the free inhabitants thereof, & amongst others of the said priviledges, there was granted unto the General Assembly of said Colony, full power & authority to make & ordain laws suiting the nature, & constitution of the place, in particular to direct, rule & order all matters relating to the purchase of lands of

the native Indians ; And this present Assembly taking into
their serious consideration that the lands of the several
Towns of Newport, Providence, Portsmouth, Warwick &
Westerly were purchased by the several inhabitants thereof
of the native Indians, chief Sachems of the Country, before
the granting of the said charter, so that an order or direction
from the said Assembly could not be obtained thereon, and
it having been thought necessary and convenient for the reasons aforesaid, that the lands of the aforesaid towns should
by an act of the General Assembly of his Majesty's Colony
be confirmed to the inhabitants thereof, according to their
several respective rights and interests therein ; Be it therefore enacted by this present Assembly, &c., That all the
lands lying & being within the limits of each & every of the
aforesaid Towns of Newport, Providence, Portsmouth, Warwick & Westerly, according to their several respective purchases thereof, made & obtained of the Indian Sachems, be,
& hereby is allowed of, ratified & confirmed to the *Proprietors,* of each of the aforesaid towns, and to each & every of
the said *Proprietors* their several & respective rights and
interests therein, by virtue of any such purchase or purchases
as aforesaid : to have & to hold all the aforesaid lands by virtue of the several purchases thereof, with all the appurte-
nances, &c. to them belonging, or in any wise appertaining,
to them the aforesaid Proprietors, their heirs, & assigns forever,"—"in as full large & ample manner to all intents, con-
structions & purposes whatsoever, as if the said lands &
every part thereof had been purchased of the Indian Sachems
by virtue of any grant or allowance obtained from the General Assembly of this Colony after the granting of the aforesaid charter ; And whereas there is within several of the
Towns within this Colony, considerable of lands lying yet in
common or undivided, & for the more orderly way & manner
for the several Proprietors—their managing the prudential
affairs thereof, & for the more effectual making of just &
equal division or divisions of the same, so that each & every
of the *Proprietors* may have their true & equal part & proportion of rights & that the exact boundaries of each &
every man's allotments when laid out to him, may be kept

in perpetuum. It is further ordered & enacted by the authority aforesaid, that it shall & may be lawful for the *Proprietors* of each & every such Town within this Colony being convened by a warrant from under the hand & seal of an Assistant, or Judge of the Peace in such Towns — the occasion thereof being specified in the warrant—for them or the major part of them to meet, to choose or appoint a clerk, &c., a surveyor or surveyors, &c., & such or so many other officers as they shall judge needful & convenient for the orderly carrying on and management of the whole affairs of such community, and in like manner to proceed from time to time as need shall require. And it is further ordered that each & every town within this colony shall & hereby are fully Impowered to make & ordain all such acts or orders for the well management Rule & ordering all prudential affairs within their or each of their respective bounds & limits as to them shall seem most meet & convenient. Always provided, & in these cases, such acts & orders are not repugnant or disagreeable to the laws of the Colony."

Other sections of this act provide for the other towns. Everything is here confirmed and made valid as the Proprietors desired. All objections to the sachems' titles were now removed, never to be heard again.

The Proprietors were now a corporation. They could act by majorities—could no longer be controlled or visited by the town meeting, but only by the Legislature, which was full of the representatives of towns having corporations like their own. They were now popularly styled "The Proprietors." The name of "Purchasers," referring to an event long passed, became obsolete. They could divide their estate at their own pleasure. The lands "up streams without limits " were assured to them, and no courts could question their title, or suggest any constitutional scruples.

The corporation made no change in its policy or its methods. They still discouraged all pursuits but those of farmers, as they had done from the beginning. Thus, December 14, 1681, "All inhabitants or strangers are prohibited from making coale or tar from pitchwood, &c., except to the quantity of ten gallons for his own use." [*ex. gr.* see

February 24, 1661.]   It had been the old practice of the
town, during the summer, that the "people" (*i. e.*, the freeholders) were allowed to pasture their cattle in "Providence
Neck,"* "paying for the damage that they doe."   This was
still permitted.   On the 17th of July, 1682 (p. 65), an order
of the town meeting recites that "Many persons to ye greate
damage of ye Towne & of every commoner therein, through
their covetousness, do irregularly & at unreasonable times, cut
ye thatch, growing upon ye towne's common, thinking to
benefit themselves, and to damnifie ye commons belonging
to ye towne, and thereby in a little time will ruinate the
same to ye Towne's great damage."   The penalty was a
forfeiture of all the thatch so cut and ten shillings for every
load, to be paid to the town treasury.   This annoyance lasted
through several generations.   Against these offenders the
authority of the law could be successfully invoked, as the
thatch-beds were in full view of the "Towne Streete."   [See
Town meeting Records, July 27, 1704.]   Swine and goats
were the chief pests of the eary Proprietors, who, in spite of
all their prohibitions, saw these reckless marauders wasting
their meadow lands.†

(At this time, A. D. 1682, the west side of the "Towne
Streete" was not built up.   The houses on the east side of
it stood upon a high bank looking down upon the shore and
over the waters of the cove, 7th April.   July 27th, 1704,
Daniel Mathewson of Providence, for £30 conveys lands on
"the south side of the salt water cove which lieth before
the row of houses in said Providence Towne.")

Their orders were time and again renewed and revoked.
The people resisted the forfeiture of a valuable part of their

---

*Before the division of the town of Providence, that part of it lying
between the Seeckonck and the Mooshassuc was called in deeds and
records "Providence Neck."

†A new generation has now grown up which remembers nothing
of the ancient thatch-beds on the north side of the cove, and on the
banks of the Wanasquatucket.   They were once among the most valuable possessions of the Proprietors, yielding a sure income.   Their
destruction, caused by the narrowing and filling of the cove on the building of the Worcester Railroad, 1843–5, was one of the first changes in
the scenery of the old town.

subsistence and during the first century of the town its records abound with complaints of the aggressions of the small freeholders and preserve memorials of the unavailing endeavors of the Proprietors to protect their domain. Their exclusive rights, the rural freemen never learned to respect. Protection was impossible, for there was no efficient police, and the proprietary lands were everywhere unenclosed. Far on in the next century, so long as any considerable part of them remained unsold, we meet with orders like this : February 6, 1710-11, " Swine found on the common without yoke or ring in the nose, to be forfeit." In its earlier days these prohibitions, and others like them, were not without their terrors, for the town meeting was alike informer, witness and judge. Years after the Proprietors had withdrawn their affairs from its cognizance, they still, as the chief landholders, controlled its decisions. In 1710 (May 22),* they ordered that "Goates are not to go at liberty on ye common." The "goates" still supplied a large portion of the meat of the poorer citizens, who were not to be allowed to feed them at the Proprietors' expense. In 1720, geese made their appearance on the common and fell under the same condemnation. July 27, 1720. "No goose is to go upon the commons highways or waters, or on any other persons land, on penalty of forfeiture." These are a few, but sufficient, specimens of the legislation of the Proprietors for the protection of their estate. All was in vain. The freeholders persisted in cutting timber in the unguarded forests and their owners vainly threatened those who felled their oaks and pines. The swine of the freeholders made havoc of the meadows, and the narrow policy of the Proprietors left them with little sympathy or redress. The smaller freeholders furnished most of the jurors, and we may be assured that they did not incline strongly against their own brethren in a legal contest with a Proprietor. These are specimens of the ills which befell the landholders of those days. They were increased by the loss of many evidences of title, at the burning of the town. This

*We cannot blame the Proprietors. The "goates" devoured the young seedlings and after a few years their ravages would have become apparent in the total disappearance of the forests. It was fortunate that other meats became plentiful before this mischief was done.

was deplored by Thomas Olney at the town meeting of
1684, as a cause of many succeeding troubles.   Boundaries in the wilderness were irrecoverably lost, and a re-ad-
justment could only be effective after a long and irritating
controversy of Proprietors with freeholders, or with each
other. In those early days wealth had its anxieties as well as
now. Some of these arose from unskillfulness or want of
care, as thus : March 17, 1683-4. By a vote of this day it
appears that the business of the draught of the 150 acres on
the west side the seven-mile line was so imperfect that "each
man's turn cannot be known," "by reason that several
names are wanting, by which it cannot appear that they ever
had any draught," and "some appear named more than once,
as if they had two draughts, and some twice numbered." Let
us not enquire the name of the town clerk of those days or
why the landholders paid so little attention to their titles.
We may not blame them if they deemed the property to be
of little value. We may be content to learn that the whole
draught was declared void and null, and that a second
draught was ordered to be made.*

It might be of interest to say something of the methods
and amount of taxation by which those early freemen maintained their social order. It is not now possible to give any
full account of it, the papers of the town treasurer having
shared the fate of the other documents of the old town.
Great irregularities in levying and collecting taxes were common during the first century of the town. June 13, 1681, *ex.
gr.* "John Whipple chosen Moderator .   .   . Whereas our
Magestrates, with some others, took upon them to make a
rate (as it is said by Town order) and have rated such as by

---

*December 2, 1685. On a question being made as to an order about
lands, made in 1658, concerning all the lands on the west side of the
Mooshassuc, it is recited that "said order by reason of damage which
our town records sustained in the late Indian War hath miscarried."
July 27, 1686. A title which had once been recorded was ordered to be
again recorded from the recollection of the town clerk, who asserted that
" he had seen it." 1678. Daniel Abbott desires to transfer a return of
his land into the new book from the old, which is "much defaced by the
Indians, 'for the more security.'" His request was granted by the
town meeting.

Town's order they had not to doe to rate, some being not freemen, some widdows, & some other. Voted by ye towne, that no person or persons whatsoever, shall be rated to pay Sergeant's wages or houserent, that are not free*men* of this towne, or have paid their equal proportion to each of them or any of them that they have paid : any order to ye contrary hereof in any wise not withstanding."*

SOME FRAGMENTS ILLUSTRATING THE GROWTH OF THE TOWN UNDER THE RULE OF THE OLD PROPRIETARY MEETINGS.

December 28, 1681. "Voated by ye Towne that there be a sufficient highway kept for ye Towne's use, of 3 poles wide from ye towne streete to ye waterside, that ye Towne if they see cause, may set up a warfe at the end of it, in the most convenient place that may be, and in order thereunto, the two surveyors & Thomas ffield are appointed to state the place & lay it out, and make return to ye Towne Meeting, ye next Quarter day or as soon as they can doe it." This was by the town, but it needed the assent of the Proprietors before any of their own land could be taken. This was a local improvement designed to give access to the "meadows of Weybossett." The "warfe and ferry" long preceded the bridge. The ferry-boats plied between the "towne streete and Weybossett Street ;" all the intervening distance has been filled up in modern times. The Proprietors had land enough yet undivided and unimproved on the west side of the river, but let them have the credit of this bit of enterprise.

Under the narrow and rigid rule of a society like this, enterprise became impossible. If any of the young men were infected with it, their only resource was to seek a habitation elsewhere. There was no reason why Providence should not have found in the fisheries and in navigation greater diversity of occupation and breadth of ideas. Its maritime advantages were equal to those of Salem, of New-

---

*Any consideration of this subject would occupy too large a space and lead us too far from our present subject.

buryport, or of New London, all active in nautical adventure from the beginning ; but at the close of the seventeenth century, when the town had some fourteen hundred inhabitants, there was not among them the owner of a single sea-going vessel. The proprietary estate had been in many ways a heavy burden. The sons of those who had rejected the enlightened project of Williams, now began to perceive that they had only postponed the day of their own prosperity. As they rid themselves of swamp and meadow, rocky and upland, the townsmen began to study the resources of the Bay. For sixty years few had joined them but beside occasional purchasers of small farms. Such was the only property offered in the market of Providence. After Philip's war, some saw there were other and better things within their reach than the Indian liquor trade, so vigorously denounced by Williams. It was in the power of the townsmen to encourage other forms of industry, by promoting iron-works, and the production of naval stores. But the older generation still desired none of these things, and consulted only what they conceived to be their own interests, by sales to approved emigrants, or by dividends of lots among themselves.* Their policy was uniform and consistent. So late as 1662, the town meeting had ordered that, "no person whatsoever, whether townsmen or other shall carry or cause to be carried either directly or indirectly off the Commons any fencing stuff, butts, pipe-staves, *clayboards* (sic), shingles, pitch-lights, or any other sort of building timber out of this Plantation, without leave of the town ;" and a heavy penalty was provided for the transgressor. This was a virtual prohibition of shipbuilding. The first Proprietors — all farmers — had no desire to encourage the foreign or even the coasting trade. So it was still. Twenty years later they adhered to the same policy. Gabriel Bernon, a shipowner and merchant, proposing to set up the manufacture of naval stores, desired for that purpose a lease

---

*The Proprietors *sold* lots to their own members on the same terms as to others, but when the lots were *given freely*, it was always by an equal dividend to each one of them. This had been an old custom. It was re-affirmed by the Proprietors on the 6th of March, 1693-4. They then voted that no individual Proprietor should have any land laid out for himself, but that an equal allotment should be made to all.

of pine woods near Pawtucket. In that age of maritime adventure and war, Boston men were growing rich by shipment of masts, spars, tar, and turpentine to England. Why should not Providence have a share in the profit? But the Proprietors in control of the town meeting peremptorily refused the request. This was their resolution on January 27, 1703-4 : "Whereas Mr. Gabriel Bernon exhibited a bill desiring of this Towne to grant him the use of all the pine trees on the black hill, & from thence to Pawtucket River, within our Plantation, to leake them and make pitch of the turpentine, & also grant him 20 acres of land near that place. The Towne did not see cause to grant the bill."

They were not all equally narrow in their views, and some of the younger Proprietors occasionally joined with the freeholders in thwarting their associates. But still the older Proprietors maintained their authority, while the influence of the seventeenth century ruled the town. There were occasional signs that a new generation was growing up.

As the ordinary freeholders increased in numbers, they made new aggressions upon the lands of the Proprietors west of the seven-mile line. The number of Proprietors was still limited to 101, and their means of self-protection did not improve. They built no houses, made no leases, gave no sites to the town, and derived their income only from their sales. This age has been accustomed to regard its small landholders as a conservative body. It was not so in New England in the seventeenth century, as it is not in Old England of the nineteenth. Some of these saw that if Providence hoped to gain any rank among the New England towns, it must find some other occupation besides that of quarreling over its land titles. As the old generation slowly disappeared, whose names ever are associated chiefly with these local strifes, topics appear in the town meeting book which had found no mention in former days. It is only from fragments like these that the history of the Proprietors can be traced, when the writings of Fox and Williams aid us no more.

During their earlier years the Proprietors gave little of their estate to any purposes of public benefit. The first of these was the Town Mill, which, however, was a necessity of their own as well as of the freemen at large. They made no improvements and gave no aid to those who would make them, even though it might promote the increase of the town. In order to promote decorum in public meetings, Williams had desired to separate the town meeting from the tavern which had been its only shelter. To this end, he offered to make a contract with the town to erect a building of convenient size. His project was for a time entertained, but, through what influences we know not, before it could be effected, the Proprietors or town meeting discharged and released him from his undertaking without coöperation or thanks. (See January, 1666, Early Records of Providence, Vol. III., p. 92.) They gave no aid to this useful design either of lots or timber, and it was not revived during sixty years. In 1695-6, Quarter day, January 27th, some of the more enlightened inhabitants asked of the town meeting a "spot of land," as they called it, "to set a schoolhouse on," about the highway called Dexter's Lane, or about Stamper's Hill. The Proprietors authorized them to take forty feet square, but offered no building material, which would have been more valuable, and left the benevolent projectors to accomplish the work as they might. They were not successful. The fathers of the town never perceived that small gifts from their estate would have increased the value of the whole domain. They gave no aid of lots or timber for the building of wharves or bridges or public works, nor allowed any one to fell trees for such uses. They waited for other men's improvements to make their own estate more valuable, while it was still exempted from the taxes which were borne by the rest of the community. Long after the beginning of the eighteenth century, so long as they met with the town meeting, at which they wielded the power of the town, they denied residence in it to every one who did not please their fancy. One or two examples may suffice : "At a Town Meeting, Quarter day, October 27, 1705, Thomas Olney, Moderator, Samuel Mead desired of the town to accommodate him with 'forty or fifty acres of land, or what they see cause.' The Purchasers & Proprietors having considered his bill, do not see cause to accommodate him with any land." "Samuel Ralph having desired for an accommodation of lands, but the Proprietors do not see cause to grant it." It might be thought that one who offered to buy or to cultivate fifty acres of wild land was not a useless or undesirable citizen, but in many such cases the application was rejected, apparently, for no better reason than personal dislike. [Those who would become inhabitants of the Plantations were still forced to buy land directly from the Proprietors. This alone gave them a foothold. The freemen who had already bought, seldom sold their homesteads in those days. The greater number of recorded sales were still directly from the Proprietors. The deeds were still returned by the Proprietors' surveyors and "confirmed" by the town meeting, before they could be recorded.]

The generation then living (1702) were a little more liberal. April 27, Quarter day, twenty acres were granted, but for life only, to John Tabor, "on account of the burning of his house & goods." He was an ancient inhabitant, is mentioned with respect, and was in danger of becoming a charge upon the town. But such displays of generosity were infrequent. Now that in a new generation a demand for town lots had sprung up, though it was but small, the private meetings of the purchasers and proprietors became more frequent. These were appointed at other times than those of the regular town meetings, and were only for the purpose of considering matters relating to lands. (See January 27, 1693-4.) The Proprietors had many questions before them which do not vex citizens of modern days. They enquired not merely as to the solvency of the buyer, but as to his fitness for becoming an inhabitant of the town. Such doubts were not always solved without difference of opinion and debate.

Sixth March, 1693-4. "It is ordered that after the last day of April next at the first opportunity convenient, the Purchasers' surveyor may proceed to lay out the land on the west side of the seven-mile line, 150 acres to each right, giving notice of the same, that each person may repayre to take his turne," "according to his draught or lott." Arthur ffenner had become impatient of the chances of the proceedings, and laid out land for himself. His acts were adjudged to be illegal. This dividend was ordered privately, and without consultation with the town meeting. Sales of town lots were frequent during this year. Whoever has any curiosity respecting the dividend of this year, may find the order of the Proprietors respecting it, in the records of December 28, 1694. The town was not yet very prosperous, and it was necessary to give some encouragement to craftsmen.* April 27, 1696. Thomas Olney, Moderator. . . "It is granted unto Joseph Goldsmith at his request, that he may have liberty to set up a smith's shop upon the common between Thomas Harris, his lott, and Samuel Whipple's house, provided he damnifieth not the highway." This was in the part of the town street, now called "Constitution Hill." We have many illustrations from the records that the townsmen of those days were not so delicate in their sensibility to annoyance by sights or sounds or odors as their descendants in our day. We have now sufficient evidence of the new direction in which young ambition was seeking success. April 27, 1697. Thomas Olney, Moderator. . "Whereas Arthur ffenner hath desired ye grant of a ninety foot lott on Waybossett side, near Muddy bridge, the Towne have considered his request & doe conclude that each Proprietor ought to be equal in those sort of lotts, according to proportion, & therefore doe defer ye matter to farther consideration & a way may be so considered & ordered that each Proprietor be so accommodated, there being several bills before depending for a way for like grants." The old practice was becoming burdensome. An enterprising Proprietor who wished to undertake some mercantile business must first assume the labor of procuring a general dividend, and still be uncertain whether he should draw the lot which he wanted, or that the Proprietor who had drawn it would sell it to him. Arthur ffenner had renewed the old agitation. On the 7th of February, 1697–8, a committee was appointed for a grant of "forty-foot lotts, called warehouse lotts." On the 7th of Feb-

*Had there been much demand for mechanical labor, the artificers would have come without encouragement.

ruary, 1697-8, it was ordered that the Purchasers and Proprietors meet together on the 10th of March to consider of
a division of land on the seven-mile line, and to take order for
effecting the same. " 10th of March. Ordered that each person who shall have right to land on ye west side of ye seven-
mile line, pay in 1 shilling for running ye western line of our
Plantation, before he shall have any land laid out on ye west
side of ye 7 mile line." The population was still so scattered
that the boundary was not well marked and needed renewal.
It seems that the old Proprietors were not always more
prompt in their payments than some of their posterity have
been, and that they sometimes needed to be sharply reminded
of the fact.

When lots were wanted for some use deemed public, the
town meeting, disregarding the old law, now began to help
themselves out of the Proprietors' estate, and to be charitable
at their expense. Sometimes they still permitted an influential citizen to exchange his lot for a better one. We have
already remarked upon the want of any constitutional protection to property in those days, and the Proprietors, so long
as their lots were still numerous, were careful not to risk
their popularity by refusal of a favor. A few examples will
suffice: July 27, 1699. "Whereas J. Olney hath this day
desired of the Towne to accommodate him with a lot, forty
foote square to set a smith's shop upon, & *what other use,*
may be made of the same, the Towne having considered the
bill, & in consideration that the said *John Olney* hath not land
in the town to build upon, and the town being desirous that
he should follow his trade of a smith in ye towne, doe grant
unto the said John Olney that he shall have a forty foote lott
in the Western end of the lane called Dexter's lane, neare
about the place where the stocks now stand, and so to be
laid out, as it may not damnify the highway." The family
took care of their poor relations at the public expense.

In an age of constant war and dread of French invasion,
military exercises were everywhere popular. Several training
fields were provided out of the proprietary estate, on the
west side of the town. These were not very extensive, none
of them exceeding three acres in extent. The evolutions

there performed could have caused little alarm to Canada or
to France. January 27, 1698-9. The town meeting grants
three acres for a training place. July 27, 1699, another training field was established west of the Mooshassuc. The next
year saw the most valuable gift as yet made by the Proprietors. It was proposed by Thomas Olney, doubtless with
their assent. Let it not detract from their merit and their
forecast, that this was the most barren and desolate sandhill
in the town; of which no one, during sixty years, had shown
any inclination to relieve them. In the month of June, 1700,
the North Burying Ground was established. It was to remain in perpetual common for a training field and for the
burial of the dead. Notwithstanding their declaration of
trust, the town sold a part of the land at the south end of
the field, but the city has made a more ample purchase at
the north, and its perpetuity is well assured. So conservative were the old townsmen of their primitive custom of
sepulture, that little use was made of the new cemetery during twenty years, except for military purposes. Gravestones
and monuments of any kind were then so few that it cannot
be determined when interment at the "north end" became
the usual practice of the town. Many of the old Proprietors
have there their resting places — let it preserve a kindly remembrance of one good deed of care and thoughtfulness for
those who were to follow them.

The Proprietors' town property was now in some danger of
melting away, from the liberal grants of the town meeting.
Strangers to their society who sought to enter upon mercantile pursuits which were generally declined by the Proprietors
were now presenting petitions for "warehouse lots," by the
waterside. There were long rows of these lots as yet unoccupied, in the unnamed swamp, where are now Weybosset
and Westminster streets, and on the west side of the town
street, opposite to the home lots on the east side. Buyers
were impatient of the rule of the Proprietors and the town
was standing still. The freeholders now persisted in voting
upon all questions relating to the sales of proprietary lands.
It was not always easy, in a thinly attended town meeting to
determine who the Proprietors were. They might be caught

unawares, when few of their number were present, as no previous notice seems to have been required of a motion to give away or sell one of their lots. By their liberal grants from the "commons," the freemen were threatening the security of estates which the Proprietors would not willingly suffer to pass from their control. It became necessary to divide these among themselves, if they would retain them in any form. In 1697-8, petitions for warehouse lots were becoming frequent and the slow-moving Proprietors would sell only in their own time and way. In that year they divided to each of themselves, a warehouse lot in Waybossett or in the town street. This was not by lottery, but they generally granted to each of their number the water lot opposite his homestead. These were of the width of forty feet, and little forethought or care was shown in leaving alleys between them for future access to the river. These narrow lanes are an inheritance from the old agricultural proprietors. For modern streets we are indebted to the new commercial freemen. The aggressions of this new class of townsmen did not cease, and in 1703-4, February 17th, the Proprietors carried this resolution in the town meeting. It was drawn up in this rasping and peremptory manner, by Thomas Olney, the town clerk. "Whereas several persons have exhibited bills desiring a grant to them of Warehouse lots it hath been considered that the land in this Town belongs to the Purchasers (as to what lies in common undivided), and that those persons who may legally vote in matters as to government may not have to doe to act & voate in the disposition of lands, as it may plainly appear by several passages in our Towne Records. Therefore if they are inclinable to propagate their desire (if they see cause), they may apply themselves to the Purchasers at their meeting." (The original record is in the handwriting of Thomas Olney.) The law which separated these two classes of voters marked also the social distinction which prevailed without complaint or cavil during the colonial time.

In the eighteenth century, now begun, the old "tumults" and "heats" in the town meetings came to an end. The legal *status* of the proprietary corporation was now everywhere recognized. It had only to fear the depredations of secret plunderers, who, in the absence of a police, were not easily restrained.* So late as February, 1715, the swine of the freeholders ran riot in the wood lands, which in their unenclosed condition seemed to invite attack.†

The thatch beds of coarse reedy grass, growing about the cove and along the Wonasquatucket, were, from an early period, regarded as a valuable possession by the Proprietors, and by the town. Each party had beds exclusively its own, which it guarded with jealous care.‡ In July, 1685, there had been farther efforts by the town meeting to prevent cutting the grass by any but those who were authorized by the respective owners. As the town grew larger, and the modest dwellings of those days more numerous, the loss was sensibly felt by the treasuries of both town and proprietary. The following vote (July 27, 1704), shows something of their mutual relations, at least as respected one not unimportant source of revenue. "Whereas, by several persons of this town there hath been this day, a bill exhibited to the purchasers, now met, that by them care might be taken for the orderly cutting of the thatch-grass on the thatch-beds which are within our township of Providence, so that each *Purchaser & Proprietor* in the commons belonging to & in said Township may have his proportion of the said thatch-grass according to his proportion of comon which he hath within said township, & not for those who have a smaller or lesser part or right in the comon to deprive these, of those just parts of the said thatch-grass who have a greater & more full right to ye said comons, but such purchaser or proprietor may have of the said thatch-grass proportionable according unto what his right of comon is; therefore for the propagation thereof, the Purchasers now met doe order & appoint Mr. Joseph Williams, Major John

---

*February 26, 1710–11. Swine were to be restrained from going on the commons without yoakes and rings.

†May 22, 1710. "Ordered that no goates shall be left to goe at liberty on ye common, but shall be confined within their owners' land." (So also of horses.) The number of such "voates" proves that they were not enforced.

‡July 17, 1682, a fine of ten shillings was imposed upon every one who cut the thatch-beds without authority.

Dexter & Captain Thomas ffenner, to draw up in writing, some method & way how & in what order, the matter premised may suitábly be affected and to propose it to the purchasers at their meeting on Monday the 14th of August next. In order thereunto, it is hereby ordered that the Purchasers shall meet together on Monday the 14th day of August next."* On the same day order was taken for the building of a "bridge from the Town side of the salt water in Providence Towne, adjoining against the west end of the lott where Daniell Abbott his dwelling house standeth, & so across the water unto the hill called Weybossett Hill." A committee was appointed to solicit contributions from the principal inhabitants. Like most attempts to raise money for public works by voluntary contribution, this one met with no success. The Proprietors offered neither lots nor timber, and the people waited patiently during several years to come. (The first bridge extended from the "Towne Streete," to the present opening of Weybosset Street, and the successive bridges have been shortened with the gradual filling up of the river.)

The prosperity of the Proprietors was probably not much diminished by the depredations of swine and goats. But as time went on there were new and more serious causes of apprehension. During sixty years they had been occasional sellers of small parcels of swamp and meadow. They were now the chief holders of town lots, and many freemen who were not of their society were anxious to procure homesteads for themselves and for their friends. The town was enlarging its borders. The hundred and one Proprietors had long ceased to be the majority of the town meeting, and the admonitions of Thomas Olney, that the freemen who were not of their number had no right to vote away the domain of the Proprietors, were failing of their effect. These were unwilling to provoke the resentment of the freemen, who had learned the power which the old institutions of the town gave

*It is to be feared that the limited skill and eloquence of Major Dexter and Captain ffenner were unable to restrain the householders, whose humble dwellings were in need of new roofs, from helping themselves to this spontaneous product of the earth, wherever they might find it.

them. The old law by which all deeds were invalid until they had been approved by the town meeting, was still in force. If the Proprietors were not as liberal in their gifts of lots as the popular majority desired, it was in the power of the town meeting to delay or prevent all their dividends and sales. This had been done in one instance where they had prevented a division during nearly two years, by refusing to record the deeds. The society was not desirous of any renewal of the strife. But such votes as the following were becoming rather too frequent: "On the Town's Quarter day, Thursday, January 27, 1703–4, Thomas Olney, Moderator . A lot forty feet square was granted to William Edmunds to set a blacksmith shop on it, within the space of one year from this day, the which if he fails of so doing, then the said piece of land shall return again to the Towne." This lot lay between the lands of Joseph Whipple, half-way up what is now "Constitution Hill," and the "prison-house," at the head of it. On the same day a lot forty feet square was granted by the *Town Meeting* to William Smith for a weaver's shop. The conditions were the same, to build within a year, and to follow his trade. Such votes savoured too much of the communistic theories of modern days. This was a cheap and easy method of being charitable at the expense of other people, and the resort to it was becoming more frequent. The admonition of Thomas Olney produced no effect, and in a few years the danger became threatening.

The Proprietors still clung tenaciously to their old agricultural pursuits and habits, and did not welcome the new age which was coming in. The wilderness beyond the "seven-mile line" was yielding to the axe and plough, and already afforded some little trade to the town street. It was now sought, not so much to prevent the sale of timber as to confine it as a monopoly to its chief owners.* As the Proprie-

---

*February ye 6th, 1709–10. . "It is ordered that no strangers nor any other person who is not interested in ye Common of our Plantation, of *his own right*, shall cut down, carry away, or make improvement of, any cedar or pine timber, or any other sort of Timber in our Township, or its Comon, unless they have grant from ye *body* of ye purchasers & proprietors; and if any shall presume to act contrary to this order, they

tors neither built nor improved nor enclosed, most of their corporate property outside the "town streete" had grown up into woodland. They were the chief holders of timber lands of which they desired to make some advantage in the age of navigation which was before them. The freemen showed little inclination to aid the Proprietors in guarding their estate, and as the younger and more active citizens they had learned some political devices which would have done no discredit to a later day. Thus, the Proprietors appointed a private meeting of their own, at an early hour in the morning, to make arrangements for acting in concert in the town meeting of that day. The younger men, it seems, were earlier risers than their elders, and thus thwarted their design. "At a Towne Meeting, June ye 6th, 1709. . . . The Meeting is adjourned to ye 9th instant in ye morning, before the Purchasers meeting begins."*

While the Proprietors' estate lasted, the thatch-beds were a continual source of annoyance as well as profit, and the association endeavored to rid itself of them, as they had done with the farm lands beyond the seven-mile line. This is an extract from a resolution of July 27th, 1706 : "Ordered that every particular share of said thatch-bed shall be divided out to each person who are proprietors, according to their proportion, between this day and the first of May next ensuing, and each person to pay his share of money for the *dividing*,† before he receiveth his (part ?). This part of the thatch-beds — that beyond the cove — seems to have given no farther trouble. A single owner could watch his own portion far more effectively than a committee or the agents of the Proprietors could keep guard over the whole.

But the old vexations remained. Few would trouble themselves to make, still less to enforce, laws intended solely for

shall be liable to be dealt withall in a due course of law by legal prosecution. Neither shall any person who is interested in the commons of our towne, grant leave to any stranger or give to act with any ye timber on ye towne's Commons, as aforesaid unless it be with ye consent of ye body of ye said Purchasers & Proprietors."

*Eight o'clock, A. M. was not an unusual hour for the town meeting.

†This payment was for surveyors and other expenses. They had nothing to pay for the land itself.

the benefit of the Proprietors' estate. The ravages of swine (see for example January 27, 1712) upon the unenclosed commons were again before the town meeting. The Proprietors were now a hopeless minority. They were chiefly residents of the "compact part of the town," while the freemen, their old enemies, controlled the remainder. They could now expect little from the town meeting, and could only stand on the defensive and protect themselves. They hesitated long. Thomas Olney, the second of the name, had spent all his best years in the office of town clerk. He was the depositary of the town's traditions, and knew all its land titles and its local history. He was in all things a lover and a preserver of things gone by. He had lived through its controversies and its disasters, and had learned sufficient law to guard it against serious mistakes.* He remembered the time when his father, Thomas Olney, and his proprietary brethren had been the whole town meeting. His own life had been spent in the support of their interests while they were a declining minority in numbers, and now through his sagacious purchases he was probably the wealthiest among them. He could not endure any radical change in the Proprietors' relations with their fellow-townsmen, although he knew that their political ascendency had hopelessly gone by. Such was his authority among them while he lived, that no separation could be accomplished. When he was laid to rest in the quiet of his "home lot," on the hill side, his surviving brethren yielded to a necessity which he could not or would not see. In 1718 (the precise date cannot now be ascertained), the Proprietors withdrew their affairs from the cognizance and control of the town meeting. The landed corporation now elected its own clerk and began its own series of records, by which they hoped to secure their property and perpetuate the memory of their acts.† In what form their withdrawal was signified we know not, for nothing respecting it appears upon the town book. After using the town's machinery

*In his last will he mentions "my law book called Coke upon Littleton," which had been a gift from William Harris.

†They probably believed that they could thus escape the effect of the town law which subjected all deeds to a vote of approval by the town meeting, before they could be entered upon the town records.

for their own interests, during nearly fourscore years, they parted with this curt and summary intimation that they needed it no longer. Thenceforth they set up for themselves, as a private land company.

It may surprise one who remembers their incorporation under the act of 1682, that no doubt or question was suggested as to their legal right to do this. The imbecility of the Colonial Courts of Rhode Island was never more signally manifested. But no one knew law enough in those days to make any objections. The courts were merely popular assemblages, with judges not better informed than their neighbors. The utmost which could now be feared was a hot dispute in the town meeting. The Proprietors knew well with whom they were dealing and no ill consequences followed.*

Their position after the separation from the town meeting was better than ever before. The town had not hesitated when it served its purpose to use their land as a charitable fund. But they could not transfer the lot of one private owner to another, and these aggression and gifts by the town meeting, once frequent, now came to an end. As Judge Staples has observed, the Proprietors never objected to the town's taking to itself a lot which was needed for public uses, whether permanent or transitory. Far on in the last century, the town had little corporate property of its own, excepting its bridges and wharf and a small school house — holding its public meetings at the chief inns. Its public functionaries, the town clerk, treasurer, &c., kept their offices and papers in their own houses, to the great detriment of the public archives. A temporary hospital was a sufficient provision for occasional visitations of yellow fever or small pox. The public demand for such sites was infrequent, and it was but a trifling burden on the liberality of the corporation. It was a gain to the Proprietors if the town took one of their lots and improved it, and thus made their other estates more valuable. They made no objections or claims for compensation when lands were taken for roads ; for the

*The Legislature would do nothing for Providence. The town was always unpopular, and its town meetings and its parties had little to hope for from the General Assembly.

ferry at " Narrow passage," where is now " Red Bridge ;" for
the "pest house," as they called it; the schools, the jail house,
the town wharf, the market place; the dock or "wharffe,"
whereon stands the old City Hall. (The prison lot, now the
site of the police office, was given by the Proprietors of Providence in 1753,—west of the Court House and adjoining the
cove. The jail was erected by the colony on the west end of
this lot and partly over the water. See " Staples's Annals,"
pp. 180, 201.) On the other hand, the Proprietors never built
or enclosed, or incurred any expense whatsoever. The town
meeting caused but little detriment to the Proprietors, for
the old townsmen were to the last degree frugal in their taxation and expenditure.

With this new organization, all continuous history of the
Proprietors comes to a sudden close. Through whose fault
or negligence I know not, their records have utterly perished,
not a fragment surviving to the present day. They preserved
many illustrations of Colonial usages and ways of life, which
gained in interest for the antiquary, long after they ceased
to be of value to the conveyancer. Nothing remains from
which to prepare a narrative of the decay and extinction of
the once powerful society. The records of its old adversary,
the town meeting, preserve occasional reference to its acts.
These, however, are not many. The Proprietors, as their
strength decayed, carefully avoided conflict, still more, col-
lision with the town, especially such as might provoke aggression or illwill. They ordered their sales after their old ways
and methods, living prudently upon a capital now augmenting
in value, but of which one or two generations would see the
end. (See "Staples's Annals," p. 36.) In 1718, another dividend was made, after the old fashion. One hundred and one
house lots upon the southerly and easterly sides of what is
now called Weybosset Street, and on the west side of the
"towne streete," extending northwardly beyond the site
of the late " Canal Market," and on the south side of
"Olney's Lane," were distributed, one to each Proprietor's
share. All these lots seem to have been accounted as of
equal value. The centre of the town was then at the north
end, near the Town Mill and the bridge at Wapwaysett, now

Randall Street. The land on the west side of the "towne streete," north of "Mile-end Cove," was platted and divided into "warehouse lots." In most cases, these were sold by the Proprietors to the owners óf the houses opposite, on the east side of the street. Other lots were sold freely to such as desired them. Sometimes a dividend was made to each "purchase right," or share. The site of his lot was left to each Proprietor to choose for himself. As of old, it was then surveyed by the Proprietors' surveyor, allowed by the Proprietors and recorded by the Proprietors' clerk. Many of those who bought from them, did not regard their records as a sufficient security, and caused their deeds to be again recorded in the books of the town clerk. Through sales and dividends, most of the lots upon the chief thoroughfares now passed into private ownership. But so late as June 6th, 1757, it is mentioned, with apparent dissatisfaction, in the town records, that very much land in Providence Neck was still unenclosed and unsold.

The association had now entered upon its best and most prosperous days. During the third decade of the last century, the nominal price of a lot in or near the towne street, was £30 or £32; as large a nominal sum as Williams had received for the whole purchase, a century before. The commercial period of the town had begun. Houses of two stories in height were now everywhere superseding the humble dwellings of the primitive land owners, and Spanish sugars, wines and cloths from the West Indies and the Spanish main were offered in the shops of the town street.

The Proprietors were still the chief land owners and their title deeds the most numerous. During the first half of the last century, a "Proprietor's share" seems to have been one of the most valuable inheritances in Providence, its capacity for yielding nourishment being far from exhausted. With the old generations old controversies had passed away. A new cause of irritation from without had united the Proprietors and the freeholders. The new freemen, beyond the "seven-mile line,"—the successors of the "25 acre men" of former days,—kept alive their old griefs and avenged them upon the men of the town street — Proprietors and freeholders alike. The commercial interests of the town now formed a compact union to oppose the issue of illimitable reams of paper money, by which the country party sought to relieve its own improvidence and insolvency at the expense of the honor and credit of the colony. The real money — so much as there was of it — was in the "compact part of Providence Town," and the country sought, with too much success, to thrust its own burdens upon its old enemies.

During many years the never-failing topic of the thatch beds near the cove and the river valleys was the chief point of contact of the Proprietors with the town meeting. This coarse, reedy grass always yielded some revenue, and was of some interest to that economical assembly. Some of those thatch beds had been claimed by the town and had been yielded to it by the Proprietors, and so in other years, but when or how, cannot now be ascertained. During the last century their rental or income had a conspicuous place in the town's accounts. Thus : 30th of August, 1748. "It is voated & ordered that Richard Waterman, Town Clark, do let, & lease out the Town's lands, at the place called the Grate Point in Providence, to the highest bidder, for the space of seven years, & that he sign & execute a lease to such persons as he shall agree with, and that he sign such lease on behalf of the Town." Last Tuesday of August, 1769: "The thatch at the Great Point & high bank, sold to James Angell for twenty four shillings lawful money." 1767, 6th of July: "The thatch belonging to the Town, sold this day in open Town Meeting to Knight Dexter for £65, old tenor."

There are not many now remaining among us who remember the old " Grate Poynt." It was a long and not unpicturesque "cape," as the boys called it who flocked thither, fresh from their geographies, for their daily swim after school hours. The "cape" projected into the cove in a southerly direction, and was still overgrown with the ancient thatch grass. The water was clear and pure, and afforded to a long succession of school boys our first lessons in aquatic exercises. The "cape" disappeared when so large a portion of the cove was filled up for the building of the Worcester Railroad, 1843-44.

The thatch beds had their historical associations. They were the last remnant of the reserve for which Williams fought so stout a battle. With the separation of the proprietorship from the town meeting came the end of the "reservation" which he had fondly hoped would be a refuge for persons "distressed for conscience." We have seen that though the early Proprietors assented to a reservation for the use of the townsmen, they would never consent to its appropriation to any particular class, and never gave to Williams or Clarke authority to make such an offer in England. (See Town Meeting Records, Vol. IX., p. 278.) It appeared by the Proprietors' Records, that in 1658 a tract of land containing a thousand acres or more "was stated perpetually to be & lie in common," embracing a large part of what is now North Providence and terminating with the hill north of the cove and Great Point. This order was lost or it miscarried because of the Indian War. The Proprietors' meeting on the 2d day of December, 1685: "In view of the necessity of some lands perpetually to be & lie in common, near unto our Town, for the use and benefit of the *inhabitants*, enacted & ordered, that all the tract mentioned afore, which was then in common, should forever remain & be in common, & that all parts of said tract which were then taken up by any person which should at any time be laid down to common, should continually so remain;" which order was declared "irreversible without the full & unanimous consent of the whole number of the Purchasers."* It appeared by the Proprietors' records that, notwithstanding this order, at a Proprietors' meeting, 13th March, 1724, a committee was appointed by the Proprietors to divide the said stated common among the Proprietors themselves. This committee wasted no time, and on the 15th of June, reported a division and a plat. This plat was accepted, allowed and confirmed by a clear vote and lots drawn for the different shares. Upon the examination of this plat there appeared to have been left a small piece of land (the southern and eastern extremities of Great Point) undivided, of which the town kept possession as part of the

---

*This was a very common formula in those days and not very much regarded.

common stated in 1658, until the year 1747, leasing it and
receiving the rents, issues and profits.   On the 18th of May,
1747, a vote was passed by the Proprietors for the sale of
this land, and a committee was appointed who sold it to Noah
Whipple for £57, old tenor.   It appears (Town Records Vol.
IX., p. 279) that at the next term of the Inferior Court of
Common Pleas for the County of Providence, an action of
trespass and ejectment was brought by Noah Whipple
against John Whipple, then in possession as lessee of the
town, by lease dated 29th of January, 1740-1.   There was a
verdict for the defendant on a plea of possession.   The plain-
tiff did not enter or prosecute any appeal.   From that time
until 1821 it appears from the votes of the town and from
the conveyances of adjoining lands, that the town are the
owners of a piece of land situate at that place.   This is a
specimen of the confusion which existed in divers places as
to the town's and the Proprietors' property.   It was due to
the ignorance of both bench and bar in those days.   When
any such matter came to a practical issue, the Proprietors
generally had the worst of it.   The exact quantity of the
above tract the town's committee in 1823 could not ascertain.   But it appears that the town had a right to about five
acres.   The heirs of Nathaniel Smith of Providence were in
possession of part of the said five acres, being about one and
three-quarters, and the heirs of John Brown claim two acres.
Said Smith and Brown and their grantees had been in possession of the said lands for a long time previous.   The value
of the land is not sufficient to warrant a suit for its recovery
by law.   (From a report of a committee appointed by the
town meeting, August, 1823—Vol. IX., Town Meeting Records, pp. 279-80 — to examine the title to the thatch beds
belonging to the town.)   The late Judge Staples was one of
that committee.   He was the Proprietors' clerk and furnished the extract, one of the very few which remain, from
their book of records.   One and one-quarter acres were all
that was left undisputed.   Thus ended a far-sighted project
for the public good, which Williams had conceived with perhaps not well-considered benevolence, and which the first
generation of Proprietors had left as their chief contribution

to the charities of the town. Whatever hopes there may have been of parks or pleasure grounds, or gifts to public utility, have long since faded away. (See Town Records, Vol. IX., p. 265; see Book of Plats, Weybosset Street to the water.)

The third generation of Proprietors divided all into small allotments for themselves. They were suffered to do as they pleased, with but little dissent, as the wealthy landholders of those days generally were. They probably wondered at the enmity which they sometimes excited.

This is the last dividend of which any record remains. The courts of that day knew nothing of trusts or of the manner of enforcing their execution. Through their ignorance this poor remnant was all which remained of the liberal reservation by the first Proprietors for the benefit of the town which they had planted.

Their history has few more recorded incidents. Other interests had surperseded theirs in the regard of a new generation. From 1730 to 1760 their sales were frequent and profitable. A "Proprietors' share" was still one of the best inheritances in the Plantations. Descendants of Browns, Arnolds, Olneys, Angells and Watermans, found, year by year, new reasons for blessing the memory of their exiled ancestors, and were consoled for their fathers' sufferings by substantial dividends from their estates. The seven-years' war (1756–1763), like most others, created an artificial prosperity. It crowded the wharves of Providence with prizes taken by privateers, and the temporary excitement caused some demand for house lots in a day in which nothing was known of bonds or shares. This was followed by the usual torpor and stagnation. The Revolution paralyzed commerce. According to the late Mr. Howland, not a single house was built here during seven years. As the years went on, the lessening number of their deeds, and the more obscure character of the property conveyed, indicated that their capital was wasting away. Their conveyances, which filled so large a space in the earlier volumes of the town records, now become comparatively few, and at the end of the century almost disappeared. After the revival of the commerce of the town, with the wars of the French Republic and Empire, an occasional deed may be found on record, but the corporation of Proprietors was the great landholder no longer. Young men of a new generation — the last which had any participation in their affairs — were now coming into public life. One of these was the late Governor Philip Allen. He represented a Proprietors' share, which had long been held by his family. He was fond of local history and carefully preserved its details. He attended the meetings of the Proprietors until the last. The business of the society steadily decreased, and they made up for its comparative unimportance by the time which they occupied in doing it. There came to their assemblies men whose births had been registered in the early decades of the last century. These brought their recollections of old events, customs and traditions, and who gave their youthful memories of ancient men who in their own early days had seen Williams, Harris, and the patriarchs of the town. The old corporation had as much the appearance of an antiquarian or historical society as of an assembly for business. When the colonial generation had passed away, the periodical meetings had little value or interest for the younger members, who had active employment of their own. They were still held, but the life of the society was ended. There was still some remnant of its old prestige. So late as 1815 it had still sufficient vitality to maintain its right against the town in its share of the ancient thatch beds. (Town Meeting Records, Vol. VIII., p. 348.) Monday, July 24th, 1815, a committee was appointed to fix the bounds of the thatch beds above Weybosset bridge with those of the Proprietors.

There were possibilities of dormant or contingent rights, which the corporation might assert against the town or against private citizens. Nearly seventy years ago some attempts of this kind were made, chiefly under the direction of Mr. Philip Crapo, then a well-known practitioner at the bar. His claim was, that the town had taken Dorrance Street, or a part of it (formerly called Muddy dock), without compensation to the Proprietors. Other dormant claims to lands which had been appropriated by the town, would have been revived, if this had been successful. But all such hopes proved delusive. Those who remember the late Mr. Crapo, his grotesque appearance and his peculiar style of oratory, will appreciate the fact that he met with little success in awakening public sympathy for a cause in itself sufficiently unpopular.   Courts were not more favorable to it than the public from which the jurors were to be drawn.   Soon after the failure of these attempts, the Proprietors' meetings altogether ceased.   The last, of which there was any record, was in 1832, and then this ancient chronicle of grievances and hates was finally and forever closed.

The freeholders were now the owners of every valuable acre and waterfall.   Little remained which was of sufficient value to justify the expense of litigation.   During the earlier years of this century, the Proprietors' plats were in frequent requisition in the law suits about boundaries with their monuments of black-oak trees and heaps of stones of which the rural landholders were so fond.   The bounds of the Proprietors' surveyors had lacked every requisite of permanence, while estates had descended from father to son, during several generations. When the original monuments had decayed, the landholders could set their stone walls as they pleased, without consulting the Proprietors, who had no funds to expend upon lawsuits.   If any swamp, then regarded as useless, or rocky upland not worth cultivation yet remained unsold, the statute of possession has long ago confirmed the adverse title of its occupants, and the society and its claims are at rest together.   It might be difficult to determine when it became extinct. The late Judge Staples was the last holder of the once dignified and influential office of Proprietors' clerk. In his time it had sadly shrunken and shrivelled from its ancient importance.   He was little more than a guardian of its records and a preserver of its traditions.   During his long professional life he carefully protected its remains.   In his "Annals" he made no mention of its faults, and passed over without reference what he could not defend or eulogize.   He left no successor.   No antiquarian has sought to preserve the memory of the "Proprietors" since he, their last mourner, was borne to the grave.

This is a summary, I hope not an unfair or partial one, of the progress and end of the old "Society of the Proprietors of Providence," its earliest corporation once powerful, but now almost unknown. What good it may have done, I have endeavored to mention in its time and place. The work was not burdensome, for their deeds of benevolence were few and far between. Their public services did not justify their original possession of the entire freehold of the town or their subsequent incorporation by the State (1682). They never rose to the perception that even liberal gifts of their unsold acres to purposes of public utility would have hastened the growth of the "Plantations," and thus have been more profitable than a dividend among themselves. All that they accomplished had been better done by the town itself. Some long-enduring estates grew up to the comfort of private families, but little was done to promote the education or well-being of a community which had begun with no other capital. The one hundred and one had successfully grasped nearly the whole of the original purchase, by which Williams had hoped to supply the want of private wealth. They built no monument to themselves. Whoever passes through our streets to-day, and asks for the memorials of the planters of the town, will find no park or school or structure, or public work, or gift to charity or learning, for which their successors owe any gratitude to them. In the days of their prosperity they forgot to do any thing for the town which they had planted, and it in like manner has forgotten them.

GENERAL INDEX.

Abbott, 72
Daniel, 112, 123
Absolute Swamp, 68
Acquetneck, 1, 3
Allen, Philip, 134
Angell, 105, 133
James, 130
Thomas, 49
Apaum, 6
Aquidneck, 30
Arnold, 105, 133
Benedict, 6, 8, 11, 23, 80
William, 23, 80
Assotemewit, 6
Athens, 37
Atherton Company, 83
Baptists, 38
Bay people, 39, 40
Belleau, 56
Bernon, Gabriel, 114
Bill of, 115
Bewitt, Hugh, 22, 68
Bewitt's Brow, 68
Blackstone River, 64, 85
Boston, 20, 33, 42
Brown, 105, 133
Chad, 19, 23, 39, 65, 68, 72, 79
Henry, 49, 96
John, 90, 132
Burnyeat, 99
Burrillville, 87
Burrough, William, 49
Canada, 120
Canonchet, 104
Canonicus, 1, 5, 6, 8, 13, 79, 80
Carpenter, 105
Ephraim, 105

Charles I, 47, 52
Charles II, 76, 106, 107
Charter, Earl of Warwick, 32, 34
Church, 10, 11
Clarke, John, 56, 63, 76, 95, 131
Clawson, John, 46, 47, 78
Clemence, Thomas, 50, 100
Clement, Thomas, 49
Coddington, 58, 71, 77, 80, 98
Colonial Assembly, 88
Commissioners, general court of, 73
Common, 78
"lands," 24, 26, 43, 91
"lots," 47, 50
"Confirmation," 8
deeds, 80
Connecticut Colony, 9, 29, 57, 58, 81, 88
Constitution Hill, 81, 124
Cotton, John, 55
Court of Trials, 77, 97
Coweset, 104
Cranston, 55, 87
Crapo, Philip, 134
Cromwell, Oliver, 52, 58, 62, 73, 75
Dean, 73
Deeds, 47, 52, 79, 80, 89, 90, 94, 124, 133, 135; see Initial Deed.
Democracie, 37, 40
Dexter, Gregory, 22, 28, 39, 45, 53, 58, 66, 67, 68, 70, 71, 72, 78, 81, 90, 94, 96, 99, 100
John, 123
Dexter Asylum, 17
Dexter's Lane, 116, 119
Disposers, 21
Dorchester, Mass., 46, 81

(137)

Dyer, 58
Edmunds, William, 124
Ellis, James, 15
England, 1, 2, 7, 22, 26, 31, 32, 37, 38, 39, 56, 58, 62, 66, 69, 72, 74, 115, 131
Europe, 62
" Family of Love," 62
" Fellowship of vote," 14, 88, 93, 105
Fenner, Arthur, 49, 83, 90, 94, 95, 96, 99, 101, 102, 104, 117, 118
    John, 48
    Thomas, 123
Field, 59
    John, 23, 59, 72, 113
    William, 48
Field's Point, 17
Fifth Monarchy men, 62, 63
Fifty-acre division, 93
First Memorandum, 14
Foote, 60
    Joshua, 105
Foster, 87
Four-mile line, 93, 103
Fowler, Henry, 60
Fox, 99, 115
    George, 98, 99
Fox's Hill, 3, 48
France, 1, 120
Freeholders, 1, 19, 53, 59, 65, 67, 69, 71, 91, 93, 94, 96, 98, 99, 100, 111, 112, 115, 120, 122, 129, 135
Freemen, 36, 113
General Assembly, order of, 95
Glocester, 87
Goatom, 50
Goldsmith, Joseph, 118
Gorton, 28, 29, 31, 34, 36, 96
    Samuel, 27, 30
Grate Poynt, 130
Hale, Sir Matthew, 52
Harris, Thomas, 49, 118
    senior, 88, 104
    William, 1, 5, 6, 7, 8, 9, 16, 17, 18, 19, 20, 24, 25, 28, 31, 32, 35, 39, 45, 46, 53, 57, 58, 59, 60, 63, 65,

Harris, William, 71, 73, 74, 75, 76, 77, 82, 83, 88, 93, 94, 95, 96, 99, 100, 105, 106, 107
    " booke " 74, 75, 76, 77
Harrison, 62
Hawkins, William, 92
Hipsie's Rock, 68
Holland, 1
Holmes, Obadiah, 31
Home lot, 50, 51
Hopkins, Thomas, Sr., 96
Howland, 133
Hudson, William, 105
Initial Deed, 12, 14, 16, 18, 19, 20, 53, 54, 66, 67, 79, 88, 89
Inman, Edward, 48
Jenckes, Daniel, 105
    Joseph, 105
Johnston, 87
Kingsmen, 75, 76, 77
Land records, 47, 52
Leare, Jane, 48
Lime rocks, 93
Line, see Four and Seven.
London, 2, 28, 73
Manton, Shadrack, 96
Mashapog, 8
Massachusetts, 1, 2, 3, 4, 6, 7, 10, 12, 18, 22, 23, 27, 28, 29, 30, 31, 33, 34, 37, 38, 39, 40, 43, 47, 53, 55, 57, 58, 75, 80, 82, 83, 85, 105
Mathewson, Daniel, 110
Matteson, James, 49
Maushapauge, town of, 5
Mead, Samuel, 116
Meeting-house, 11
Memorandum, first, 5
    second, 6
Miantonomi, 5, 6, 8, 13, 31, 80
Moosh River, 13
Mooshassuc, 3, 4, 5, 9, 11, 12, 17, 19, 21, 22, 27, 28, 34, 37, 39, 40, 41, 55, 59, 61, 69, 74, 82, 83, 85, 91, 104, 105, 107, 112, 120
    Colony, 2
Musuassacutt Country, 83

Nanhegansett Sachems, 83
Nanhegansick, 5
Narragansett, 2, 7, 104
    sachems, 82
    wigwams, 9
Narragansetts, 1, 10, 11, 22, 65, 104, 107
Narrow passage, 128
Neuticonkanet, 5, 8, 49
Neuticonkonitt Hill, 86
New England, 43, 56, 61, 115
New Jersey, 56
New London, 114
New York, 37, 61
Newburyport, 114
Newport, 3, 12, 29, 34, 35, 58, 80, 82, 94, 107, 108
    Assembly, 96, 97, 98, 99
    act of, 107
Nipmucks, 82
Niswoshakit, 82
North Burying Ground, 120
North Providence, 64, 131
Notakunhanet, 8, 49, 86
Notquonchanet Hill, 5
Observation Rock, 68
Olney, 105, 133
    Epenetus, 45, 104
    John, 119
    Thomas, senior, 24, 25, 32, 34, 35, 36, 39, 45, 46, 48, 53, 57, 59, 60, 60, 63, 64, 65, 72, 78, 80, 82, 83, 84, 86, 88, 93, 107
        junior, 90, 99, 104, 105, 116, 118, 121, 123, 124, 126
Pachasit River, 49
Pautuckut, 5, 6, 65
Pawtucket, 8, 68, 115
    River, 86
Pawtuxet, 6, 16, 19, 28, 29, 31, 33, 34, 65, 105
    "purchase," 19, 20, 71
    River, 6, 13, 80
Philip's War, 114
"Plaister, Sovereign," 66, 67, 69
Plantations, 1, 2, 3, 5, 117, 133, 136

Plymouth, 1, 6, 7, 30, 34, 40, 98
Pomham, 80
Portsmouth, 107, 108
Pray, Richard, 48, 49
Proprietors, 1, 15, 17, 20, 21, 23, 24, 25, 26, 27, 28, 29, 30, 31, 34, 35, 36, 38, 39, 40, 41, 42, 43, 44, 45, 49, 50, 51, 53, 56, 57, 61, 63, 64, 65, 66, 69, 71, 78, 79, 80, 81, 82, 83, 84, 85, 86, 87, 88, 90, 91, 92, 93, 94, 95, 96, 97, 99, 100, 102, 103, 105, 106, 108, 109, 110, 111, 112, 113, 114, 115, 116, 117, 118, 119, 120, 121, 123, 124, 125, 126, 128, 129, 130, 131, 133, 134
Proprietors' "association," 21
    "claim," 9, 16, 67
    meetings, end of, 135
    "rights," 23, 32
    records, 131
    "share," 129, 133, 134
    surveyors, 49
    vote of, 132
Providence, 3, 5, 6, 8, 16, 17, 21, 28, 30, 33, 34, 38, 44, 49, 58, 59, 67, 77, 79, 82, 83, 84, 89, 93, 94, 96, 97, 98, 104, 106, 107, 108, 113, 115, 122, 129
    Neck, 110, 129
    Plantations, 34, 107
    Towne, 20, 23, 32, 87, 130
Purchasers, 15, 22, 23, 87, 91, 92, 93, 94, 109, 116, 122, 125, 131
Quakers, 76, 82, 97, 100, 107, 112
Quarter Court, 33
    order of, 27, 42
Quarter Day, 92, 113, 116, 117, 124
    meetings, 44, 52, 58
Quarter-rights men, 33, 35, 36, 38, 84, 91
Quinnichicutt, 6
Quorum, 25
Ralph, Samuel, 117
Records of lands, 47, 52, 100, 101, 104
    proprietors, 126, 128, 134, 135

Reddock, 94
Revolution, 133
Rhode Island, 4, 23, 38, 40, 47, 57, 58, 63, 74, 75, 76, 80, 81, 98, 107
Colonial Courts of, 127
Rhodes, 105
Sachems' "memorandum," 5, 12, 65
Salem, 42, 45, 113
Sayles, John, 90
School-house, 116
Scott, Richard, 60
Secession, 33, 35
"Second comers," 22, 23, 32, 33
Agreement of, 22, 23
Second "memorandum," 6, 65
Seekonk, 2, 91
River, 9
Seven-Years' War, 133
Seven-mile line, 68, 87, 90, 91, 92, 93, 94, 103, 112, 119, 125, 129
Slavery, 38
Smith, Edward, 101, 102, 103
resolution of, 101, 102
Fenner, 105
John, 48
Nathaniel, 132
William, 124
Smithfield, 82, 85, 87
Soconoco, 80
Soldash 6
Solvency, 23
South Carolina, 38
"Sovereign Plaister," 66, 69, 70, 72, 78, 88, 94, 96, 99, 100
Squatter Sovereignty, 4
Stampers Hill, 116
Staples, W. R., 5, 64, 127, 132, 135
Staves, 42
Steere, John, 92
Stone, Dr., 104
Suffrage, 10
Sugar-loaf Hill, 68
Surveyors, 50, 51, 100, 109
Tabor, John, 117
Tar, 109
Thatch-beds, 110, 125, 131, 134

Throckmorton, John, 7
Timber, 42, 85, 124
Town "booke," 24, 81
Deputy, 49, 78, 79
"Fellowship," 10, 20, 21, 26, 29, 33, 35
Meeting, 11, 21, 50, 56, 59, 61, 65, 72, 78, 80, 83, 86, 107, 113, 124, 125
Order of, 83, 88, 92, 104, 114, 117, 123
Courts, 52
Town Mill, 52, 56, 78, 107, 116
"Stocks," 17, 44, 53, 54
Street, 110
Training-ground, 120
Twenty-mile boundary, 89
Twenty-five acre men, 46, 69, 71, 80, 92, 93, 94, 101, 129
Tyburn, 73
Utah, 3, 62
Vane, Sir Henry, 56, 57, 58, 62, 69, 73, 96
Verin, Joshua, 44, 45, 47, 52, 72, 104, 106
"Village Hampdens," 87
Wapuaysett, 128
Warehouse "lotts," 118, 120, 129
Warwick, 31, 74, 89, 107, 108
Waterman, 133
Richard, 49, 130
Wayunkeke, 80, 81, 85
West Indies, 129
Westerly, 107, 108
Weybossett Hill, 123
meadows of, 113
Whipple, John, 15, 32, 45, 46, 65, 66, 70, 98, 104, 112, 132
senior, 50, 81
Joseph, 124
Noah, 132
Samuel, 118
Whitman, Valentine, 90
Wickenden, William, 23, 48, 68, 72, 90
Wickes, Francis, 48

Williams, Joseph, 122
    Robert, 59
    Roger, 1-22, 24-28, 30-33, 35, 36,
      38, 39, 43, 46, 50, 51, 53-66, 68-
      86, 88, 89, 90, 92-96, 98, 99, 104-
      107, 114, 115, 116, 129, 131, 132,
      134, 136
      his first deed, see Initial
        Deed.

Williams, Roger, his second deed,
      89, 90
    Roger, 2d, 106
Winslow, Gov., 7
Winthrop, John, 3, 4, 10, 29, 30, 54,
      81
Wonas River, 13
Wonasquatucket, 64, 83, 122
    River, 5, 44, 48, 50